The
VICTORS

Overcoming Toxins
That Poison
the Believer

John R.

D1211452

ACCENT
Bible Curriculum

ADULT STUDENT
Bible Study Guide

This Bible study guide is part of an adult
curriculum designed to assist you in making
the entire Bible your guide for daily living.

John R. Cionca/Author
Judy A. Stonecipher/Managing Editor
James T. Dyet/Executive Editor
James E. Burkett, Jr./Publisher
Robert L. Mosier/Founder

Accent Bible Curriculum
Accent Publications, Inc.
12100 W. Sixth Avenue
P.O. Box 15337
Denver, Colorado 80215

CONTENTS

Lesson 1
The Believer's Adversary: Satan   5
Lesson 2
Guilty, Or Not Guilty? the Toxin of Guilt   15
Lesson 3
When the Grass Looks Greener: the Toxin of Envy   22
Lesson 4
I Can't Kick the Habit: the Toxin of Bad Habits   30
Lesson 5
Gripe, Gripe, Gripe: the Toxin of Complaining   37
Lesson 6
I Am the Greatest: the Toxin of Pride   46
Lesson 7
Changing the Truth: the Toxin of Lying   55
Lesson 8
Never Enough: the Toxin of Greed   63
Lesson 9
The Silent Treatment: the Toxin of Prayerlessness   71
Lesson 10
Thinking Like a Natural Man: the Toxin of Wrong Thinking   80
Lesson 11
Lack of Self-Discipline: the Toxin of Mismanagement   87
Lesson 12
I Did It My Way: the Toxin of Self-Indulgence   96
Lesson 13
The Believer's Helper: the Holy Spirit   104

THE BELIEVER'S ADVERSARY:
SATAN
GENESIS 3:1-8; JOB 38:4-7; ISAIAH 14:12-14; LUKE 8:1-15;
EPHESIANS 6:10-18; REVELATION 20:7-10

Learn by Heart:
"Be sober, be vigilant; because your adversary the devil, as a roaring lion, walketh about, seeking whom he may devour" (I Peter 5:8).

EVERY DAY WITH THE WORD

Monday	Satan's origin	Job 38:4-7
Tuesday	Satan's fall	Isaiah 14:12-15
Wednesday	Satan's strategy	Luke 8:1-15
Thursday	Satan's deception	Genesis 3:1-8
Friday	Satan's tempting	Luke 4:1-13
Saturday	Satan's final defeat	Revelation 20:1-10
Sunday	Satan's daily defeat	Ephesians 6:10-18

"Take your mark; get set; go!" Most people have been involved in a contest. It may have been a fun event such as a baseball game in Gym class or a sack race at a Sunday School picnic. For some, it may have been more sober competition, such as the Vietnam War.

The Bible explains that Christians are in a contest. The Apostle Paul likened this contest to a race, a wrestling match, and warfare. In his second letter to Timothy he wrote that Christians should act like good soldiers who fight to the end (II Timothy 2:3,4), like an athlete who strives for the crown (verse 5), and like a farmer who labors to see the reward of his harvest (verse 6).

Christians are not competing against one another in this contest. Rather they run and fight against an adversary who will use any means possible to see them sidelined. We are warned: "Be sober, be vigilant; because your adversary the devil, as a roaring lion, walketh about, seeking whom he may devour" (I Peter 5:8). While our competitor is superhuman, he is not omnipotent. Christians can be victors because greater is he that is in us, than he that is in the world (I John 4:4b).

The Victors is a study of how Christians can overcome common toxins used against them by the enemy. Before examining some of his specific poisons, it is profitable to consider—

C.S. Lewis said we err in two ways regarding the devil: first by thinking too much about him, as if he were omnipotent, like God; and second, by thinking too little about him, as if he were not a formidable foe.

THE ADVERSARY'S IDENTITY
(Job 38:4-7; Isaiah 14:12-14)

The Bible states that "in the beginning God created the heaven and the earth" (Genesis 1:1). The "beginning" mentioned in Genesis is the beginning of what we call space and time. God the Father, God the Son, and God the Holy Spirit existed in eternal fellowship prior to the creation. In addition, we understand from the Scriptures that God created a spirit world that was already in existence prior to the creation of the earth.

Tucked away in one of the oldest books of the Bible is a dialogue between God and Job which gives more information on the origin of angels. "Where wast thou when I laid the foundations of the earth? declare, if thou hast understanding. Who hath laid the measures thereof, if thou knowest? or who hath stretched the line upon it? Whereupon are the foundations thereof fastened? or who laid the corner stone thereof; When the morning stars sang together, and all the sons of God shouted for joy?" (Job 38:4-7).

God is eternal, but at a point in time, God created the earth, with His highest creation being

Job was written near the time of Abraham.

Commentators equate "the morning stars" and "the sons of God" as angels.

6

the formation of man in His own image. Somewhere between eternity past, and the creation of the world, however, God created angels, ministering spirits. Satan, the adversary, is one of those created spirit beings.

The Bible further reveals that some of these created spirits rebelled against God and were cast out of His presence. Apparently, some of these fallen angels are in bondage. Peter wrote: "For if God spared not the angels that sinned, but cast them down to hell, and delivered them into chains of darkness, to be reserved unto judgment..." (2 Peter 2:4). Other evil angels are not bound, but are active in their warfare against God. While they are helpless against an omnipotent Creator, they attempt to take out their wrath on the objects of His creation.

Satan is a fallen angel, and many believe his fall is mentioned in Isaiah 14:12-15. In the text this lofty creation of God rebelled through pride, seeking to be like God himself (Isaiah 14:14). This text will be studied later in lesson six, but for now it is sufficient to notice God's judgment upon the adversary: "Yet thou shalt be brought down to hell, to the sides of the pit" (verse 15). The pronouncement of judgment in Isaiah 14 and that of Ezekiel 28, appears to go beyond the kingdoms of Babylon and Tyre. Lucifer, "son of the morning," the adversary, is in warfare against the godly. His battle plans can be seen more clearly by looking at—

**THE ADVERSARY'S STRATEGY
(Luke 8:4-15)**

Satan desires to glorify himself, and he tries to

Some scholars believe that the bound angels' sin was that of the sons of God in Genesis 6:2. Others say it is not certain.

Satan's sin was pride. See Isaiah 14:12-15.

do that by tempting people to align themselves with him in the dishonoring of God. His first major strategy, therefore, is to hinder people from becoming Christians. The gospel is good news, a message offering peace with God. The adversary tries to hide that truth from people. Paul wrote: "But if our gospel be hid, it is hid to them that are lost: In whom the god of this world hath blinded the minds of them which believe not, lest the light of the glorious gospel of Christ, who is the image of God, should shine unto them" (II Corinthians 4:3,4).

While Jesus was preaching in Galilee, He told a story which is known as the Parable of the Sower. He said that a sower went out and sowed seed on different types of soil. When His disciples asked Him the meaning of the parable, He gave them this interpretation. "Now the parable is this: The seed is the word of God. Those by the wayside are they that hear; then cometh the devil, and taketh away the word out of their hearts, lest they should believe and be saved" (Luke 8:11,12). The primary meaning of the parable is that some individuals are so hardened in heart that Satan can easily remove the Word of God before it can penetrate their hearts.

The adversary's strategy is to shield the lost from the truth, and he carries out his warfare through deception. He deceived Eve in the garden, and after Christ's 1000-year reign on earth he will again be released from prison and will "go out to deceive the nations which are in the four quarters of the earth" (Revelation 20:8). He knows his fate is sealed, and he desires to bring others to destruction with him.

Similar to the adversary's strategy of hindering

Other names of Satan are noted in Revelation 12:9.

people from becoming Christians, is his strategy of hindering Christians from behaving like Christ. Satan wants to insult God, to challenge His authority, and to dishonor Him. He is delighted when a child of God chooses to follow his temptations rather than God's commands.

Satan uses many means, including the foolish words of a friend. See Mark 8:33.

When Satan seeks to hinder Christians from behaving like Christ, he often uses a threefold attack. This threefold attack is described in I John 2:15,16: "Love not the world, neither the things that are in the world. If any man love the world, the love of the Father is not in him. For all that is in the world, the lust of the flesh, and the lust of the eyes, and the pride of life, is not of the Father, but is of the world." The first attack is the lust of the flesh. Satan would entice the believer to dishonor God by yielding to the pull of the flesh, whether it be that sexual pull of infidelity or that culinary pull toward gluttony. The deceiver would try to persuade a Christian that he would be satisfied by yielding to these fleshly pulls.

The adversary's second attack employs desires that come through the eye gate. The delusion may be that the new car, nicer home, more stylish wardrobe, more prestigious job, or different spouse would be more satisfying. However, experience teaches that obedience to God is what produces satisfaction. Satan will televise in living color all that the world has to offer in his attempt to have Christians honor him rather than God.

The devil's third attack is called the pride of life. Like the others, it's a denial of God's sovereignty. Satan fell because of pride, and throughout history he has tempted people to follow his lead in sinning through pride.

Satan first used this threefold attack against

Eve in the garden. In Genesis 3 we read: "Now the serpent was more subtil than any beast of the field which the Lord God had made. And he said unto the woman, Yea, hath God said, Ye shall not eat of every tree of the garden? And the woman said unto the serpent, We may eat of the fruit of the trees of the garden: But of the fruit of the tree which is in the midst of the garden, God hath said, Ye shall not eat of it, neither shall ye touch it, lest ye die. And the serpent said unto the woman, Ye shall not surely die" (Genesis 3:1-4). Notice how the deceiver first got his foot in the door by questioning what God had initially commanded. Then his deception continued by directly challenging what God said would be the result of disobedience.

After Satan enticed Eve with the prospect of being like God, the account continues: "And when the woman saw that the tree was good for food [lust of the flesh], and that it was pleasant to the eyes [lust of the eyes], and a tree to be desired to make one wise [the pride of life], she took the fruit thereof, and did eat, and gave also unto her husband with her; and he did eat" (Genesis 3:6).

Eve was deceived into believing there was satisfaction in eating that fruit. By launching his threefold attack Satan succeeded in keeping a child of God from honoring her Creator.

A second example of the adversary's threefold attack is observed in the temptation of Christ. In Luke 4:1-13 we notice that the devil enticed our Lord to create bread when He was hungry (lust of the flesh). The adversary then showed and offered Him all the kingdoms of the world (lust of the eyes).

The deceiver's third attack was directed at the

Satan did not speak to "them," but only to the woman. Are you more susceptible to temptation when you are without support of another?

Notice how Jesus used the Scriptures in resisting the adversary.

10

pride of life when he challenged Jesus to demonstrate His deity by jumping from the pinnacle of the temple.

Whereas Eve yielded to the deceiver's temptations, our Lord Jesus was victorious over them. Victory can be ours too as we remember—

THE ADVERSARY'S DEFEAT
(Revelation 20:7-10; Ephesians 6:10-18)

This period of 1000 years is called the millennium.

Because Jesus Christ was victorious over sin and death, the ultimate destiny of the adversary is sealed. Satan will be defeated. Revelation 20:7-10 indicates: "And when the thousand years are expired, Satan shall be loosed out of his prison, And shall go out to deceive the nations which are in the four quarters of the earth, Gog and Magog, to gather them together to battle: the number of whom is as the sand of the sea. And they went up on the breadth of the earth, and compassed the camp of the saints about, and the beloved city: and fire came down from God out of heaven, and devoured them. And the devil that deceived them was cast into the lake of fire and brimstone, where the beast and the false prophet are, and shall be tormented day and night for ever and ever."

Remember the promise of I Corinthians 10:13.

While it is important to know that Satan will be ultimately defeated, each Christian is more concerned with personal, daily defeat over the adversary. God has promised that nothing can separate us from His love, not even the various ranking of spirit beings (Romans 8:38,39). Although the adversary is superhuman, he is not greater than the omnipotent Holy Spirit who resides in every believer (I John 4:4). Also, James assures us that, when we resist the devil, he flees

See James 4:7.

11

from us. As we draw near to God, He draws near to us.

In his letter to the church of Ephesus Paul illustrated the seriousness of spiritual warfare by describing it in terms of hand to hand combat. According to Paul, in order to be victorious we must use the spiritual armor God has provided for His children (Ephesians 6:10-18).

The belt of truth in Ephesians 6:14 is a readiness, a preparedness, and commitment to truthful behavior. The breastplate of righteousness is a chest plate which covers our whole inner being with the righteousness of Christ. The shoes, the gospel of peace, help us to stand firmly on the solid Rock, Jesus Christ. The shield of faith, when it is held up, wards off the adversary's fiery darts—the lust of the flesh, the lust of the eyes and the pride of life. The helmet of salvation protects our minds from false teaching, discouragement, and especially doubt.

The believer has also been given offensive weapons for spiritual warfare. Paul mentions the importance of prayer (verse 18), but the primary battle weapon is the sword of the Spirit (verse 17). The *mitira* (sword) with which Paul would have been familiar, was a short sword used in hand to hand combat. It is the sword of the Word that gives us discernment (Hebrews 4:12), cleanses us (John 15:3), makes us fruitful (John 15:7,8), equips us for every good work (II Timothy 3:16,17), assures salvation (I Peter 1:23), guarantees true success (Joshua 1:8), and fosters spiritual growth (I Peter 2:2).

The adversary will be defeated ultimately, and the adversary can be defeated daily. Satan launches chemical warfare upon believers and

Paul wrote Ephesians from prison. His Roman guard was likely his point of analogy. Read Ephesians 6:10-18.

Jesus used the Sword, the Word of God, against the adversary. See Luke 4:1-12.

tries to poison them with guilt, envy, enslaving habits, complaining, pride, lying, greed, prayerlessness, natural thinking, lack of self-discipline, and self-centeredness. While the enemy is strong and subtle, however, the believer's Helper is greater than his adversary. Ultimate victory has been guaranteed for every child of God, therefore daily victory is possible. Because believers stand in the strength of the omnipotent Spirit of Christ, daily they can be the victors.

FOOD FOR THOUGHT

"The devil's boots don't creak!"
—Scottish Proverb

NOW TEST YOUR KNOWLEDGE

Fill in the Blanks:

1. "Be sober, be _____, because your _____ _____ _____, as a roaring lion, walketh about, seeking whom he may devour."
2. "For all that is in the world, the _____ _____ _____ _____, and the _____ _____ _____ _____, and the _____ _____ _____, is not of the Father, but of the world."
3. "Ye are of God, little children, and have overcome them; because _____ _____ _____ that is _____, than he that is in the world."

Match the Following:

4. Lust of the Flesh
5. Lust of the Eye
6. Pride of Life

A. Satan's tempting Jesus to jump from the temple.
B. Satan's tempting Christ to make bread.
C. Satan's tempting of Jesus to accept the kingdoms of the world.

Answer True or False:

7. The adversary is bound, not able to hassle the Christian.
8. Satan is a deceiver and a liar.
9. God has equipped believers for spiritual warfare.
10. Christians can resist the attacks of the adversary.

2

GUILTY OR NOT GUILTY?
THE TOXIN OF GUILT
II SAMUEL 11; 12; PSALM 38:1-4; 139:23,24; JOHN 16:7-11;
I JOHN 1:7-9

Learn by Heart:
"As far as the east is from the west, so far hath he removed our transgressions from us" (Psalm 103:12).

EVERY DAY WITH THE WORD

Monday	The reality of guilt	Psalm 38:1-4
Tuesday	Example of guilt	Psalm 51
Wednesday	Forgiveness of guilt	Psalm 103:8-18
Thursday	Mercy for guilt	Psalm 130
Friday	Confession and guilt	I John 1
Saturday	Perspective and guilt	Philippians 3:10-14; 4:8
Sunday	Friends and guilt	Ecclesiastes 4:9-12; Galatians 6:1,2

To the sensitive conscience, guilt accompanies all sin.

As the Christian engages in spiritual warfare, not only will the adversary try to sideline him with depression, worry, envy, pride, and other poisons, but he will also attack the Christian with guilt. Guilt is a tool of the Holy Spirit, which He uses to direct us back to the right path. However, the adversary also uses guilt to keep the Christian from a joyful and vital relationship with Christ. Therefore it is important that we have an—

UNDERSTANDING OF GUILT
(Psalm 38:1-4; John 16:7-11)

You will find the account of David's sin in II Samuel 11 and 12.

King David knew what it was like to feel guilty. He described the torment he was experiencing after his sins of adultery and murder in these words: "O Lord, rebuke me not in thy wrath: neither chasten me in thy hot displeasure. For thine arrows stick fast in me, and thy hand presseth me sore. There is no soundness in my flesh because of thine anger; neither is there any rest in my bones because of my sin. For mine iniquities are gone over my head: as an heavy burden they are too heavy for me" (Psalm 38:1-4).

Modern psychologists would try to convince us that David wasn't really guilty. They might suggest that adultery was just a normal human drive that needed to be satisfied. Men often teach what they want to believe, but God's Word teaches the truth. David was guilty of dreadful sin.

There is a difference, however, between guilt and guilt feelings. A person will feel guilty when he violates his conscience. But sensitivity of conscience varies from person to person. A mother feels guilty over sticking her child with a diaper pin. On the other hand, neither Hitler nor Idi Amin had ever voiced feeling guilty over their atrocities. How, then, can a believer distinguish between true guilt and the feelings of guilt that may come from other sources or from the adversary?

Guilt is a feeling of shame and disapproval for violating a perceived standard. There are two aspects to guilt: objective guilt and subjective guilt. Objective guilt is real guilt, true guilt, legal guilt. An example would be breaking the laws of society or breaking one of God's laws. The individual is guilty of violating the standard, whether he feels guilty or not. Whether or not Hitler felt guilty, he was morally and legally guilty, and will be judged guilty at the great white throne judgment.

Notice how David's guilt affected him mentally, emotionally and physically.

This judgment of unbelievers is

16

described in Revelation 20:11-15.

Also see Romans 2:15.

Sometimes referred to as "common grace."

Ephesians 4:30 states: "And grieve not the Holy Spirit of God, whereby ye are sealed unto the day of redemption."

Do you feel the convicting work of the Spirit when you break God's Word?

There is also subjective guilt. This is an inner guilt of emotions, feelings of regret, remorse, shame, and self-condemnation. The feelings may be strong, or they may be mild. They may be in touch with reality (real guilt), or may be out of touch with reality (false guilt).

Guilt feelings are produced when a person contradicts his conscience. Several times in the Scripture the Bible mentions the conscience. For example, Paul says in Romans 9:1: "I say the truth in Christ, I lie not, my conscience also bearing me witness in the Holy Ghost."

The conscience is formed by four influences.

1. *The Holy Spirit.* The Holy Spirit has a general influence in the world, but He has a special ministry within the Christian. The Holy Spirit is the resident Truth Teacher in every Christian. He applies the Bible to the heart, the mind, and therefore to the conscience. Jesus said the Holy Spirit would convict the world "of sin, and of righteousness, and of judgment" (John 16:8). In addition, Jesus promised that the Spirit would guide each believer (John 16:13-15). So, the Holy Spirit builds God's standards into the Christian, thereby shaping the Christian's conscience. When a Christian sins, the Holy Spirit pricks his conscience. Confession of sin is evidence, therefore, that a person is a true Christian. If a person could sin without feeling guilty, there would be reason to believe that the Spirit was not present in that person.

2. *From significant others.* Influential people have an effect on a person's thinking, and therefore his conscience. It may be parents, school peers, friends, or TV heroes. Those influential people affect how a person thinks,

how a person's mind is actually programmed. They have a bearing on what is accepted as right or wrong. The more worldliness programs the mind, the more the individual will accept things that earlier would have pricked his conscience. Everything in society has an imprinting effect on people, but the greatest shaping is caused by people who hold the most influence upon an individual.

3. *The self.* Guilt is produced not only when a person violates a Spirit- or societal-established standard in his conscience, but also when he violates his own standards. An individual might state, "I'll finish this project by Monday," or "We'll get that wallpapering done by next Saturday," or "I should have visited Bill, but just never did." These self-established expectations, left unfulfilled, are another source of guilt.

This will vary with personality types. Perfectionists who set unrealistic goals are more open to this type of guilt.

4. *Satan.* Satan is called the slanderer. He is referred to as the accuser of the brethren. He speaks to your conscience and says, "God won't forgive you this time," or "I've met some miserable Christians, but you really take the cake."

He often attacks the believer at his particular point of weakness. A Christian may say, "God, I promise You I won't do it again," or "Lord, I vow to You that I won't do that." When the Christian again falls to that temptation, the accuser tries to keep him from confession; or, if confession is made, he tries to keep him feeling guilty.

OVERCOMING GUILT
(Psalm 139:23,24; I John 1:9)

It isn't necessary to spend a lot of time convincing a person that guilt is real. It *is* important that the Christian be able to experience forgiveness for true moral guilt and to deal accurately with guilt feelings.

The first step in overcoming guilt is to become honest with God. A person first experiences forgiveness when he acknowledges his sin and trusts Christ to be his Saviour. That open acknowledgment is essential before the free gift of grace can be received. Similarly, the Christian must maintain openness before the Spirit, being sensitive to His convicting. The psalmist's words reflect this attitude: "Search me, O God, and know my heart: Try me, and know my thoughts: And see if there be any wicked way in me, and lead me in the way everlasting" (Psalm 139:23,24).

The psalmist also spoke of God's forgiveness in Psalm 130: "If thou, Lord, shouldest mark iniquities, O Lord, who shall stand? But there is forgiveness with thee, that thou mayest be feared" (verse 3). No one could stand if God held His iniquities against him, but God has provided total forgiveness through His Son, Jesus Christ.

The Adversary desires to keep us separated from God, but we read in Scripture that nothing can keep us from God's love (Romans 8:1,33,38,39). The accuser of the brethren will try, but Christ will say "Not guilty." It is God who justifies, so he who condemns is defeated.

When you feel estranged from God, it may be unconfessed sin, but it also may be the adversary.

Guilt can be purged from the believer's life when he accepts the fact that he is not condemned, and also when he realizes that Christ intercedes for him. Hebrews 7:25 says: "Wherefore he is able also to save them to the uttermost that come unto God by him, seeing he ever liveth to make intercession for them."

Just as there is forgiveness for objective guilt, so

also there can be victory over subjective guilt feelings. When a Christian feels guilty, he should first examine the Scriptures to determine if he has broken a moral principle of God. If he is truly guilty, he must confess that sin. If guilt feelings linger, meditation on the Scriptures which express God's forgiveness is very beneficial. God does not want a believer to dwell on the negative or in the past, but rather to think on wholesome things and on Christ.

For some who are deeply troubled by guilt, the counsel of a spiritually mature friend may be required to help them realize God's forgiveness. Solomon wrote: "Two are better than one; because they have a good reward for their labour. For if they fall, the one will lift up his fellow: but woe to him that is alone when he falleth; for he hath not another to help him up" (Ecclesiastes 4:9,10). God realized that a Christian needs the support of fellow believers. It is with this understanding that Paul instructed: "Brethren, if a man be overtaken in a fault, ye which are spiritual restore such an one in the spirit of meekness; considering thyself, lest thou also be tempted. Bear ye one another's burdens, and so fulfill the law of Christ" (Galatians 6:1,2). The prayerful intercession and understanding of a friend or counselor can help the believer understand the reality of forgiveness which God has provided for him.

The adversary would like to keep the Christian from feeling guilty by hardening his conscience. He would also like to keep the Christian from confessing any sin which would hinder his fellowship with the Lord. If he strikes out on the first two times at bat, he takes another swing at the

See Philippians 4:8 for a list of the positive things upon which the believer's mind should "dwell."

Remember—to have a friend, you must be one. "A man that hath friends must shew himself friendly . . ." (Proverbs 18:24).

20

Christian by trying to keep him feeling guilty after he's confessed his sin. However, the Christian who understands Satan's strategy can experience forgiveness of true guilt and deliverance from subjective guilt feelings.

NOW TEST YOUR KNOWLEDGE

Answer true or false:

1. All guilt is from God.
2. Everyone who sins feels guilty.
3. Both the Holy Spirit and Satan convict.
4. David experienced feelings of guilt related to true, objective guilt.
5. God removes sin from the believer to the infinite measure.
6. God cannot forget our sins.
7. We only experience forgiveness of moral guilt when we agree with God about our sin.
8. Dwelling on past sin is not harmful.
9. The conscience can be programmed.
10. Christians can be helped by other believers in dealing with guilt feelings.

FOOD FOR THOUGHT

"Guilt matters. Guilt must always matter. Unless guilt matters the whole universe is meaningless."

—Archibald MacLeish

3

WHEN THE GRASS LOOKS GREENER: THE TOXIN OF ENVY

GENESIS 30:1-16; PSALM 115:1-3; PROVERBS 14:30;
MATTHEW 27:11-18; ACTS 13:42-45; ROMANS 13:13;
GALATIANS 5:26; JAMES 3:14-16; I THESSALONIANS 5:15-19

EVERY DAY WITH THE WORD

Monday	Warning against envy	Proverbs 3:31-35
Tuesday	Rachel's envy	Genesis 30:1-16,22,23
Wednesday	Brothers' envy	Genesis 37:1-11
Thursday	Sanhedrin's envy	Matthew 27:11-18
Friday	The Jews' envy	Acts 13:42-45
Saturday	Effects of envy	James 3:13-18
Sunday	Extinguishing envy	I Thessalonians 5:15-19

Learn by Heart:
"A sound heart is the life of the flesh: but envy the rottenness of the bones" (Proverbs 14:30).

It is not unusual to go to a baseball game and see young children paying more attention to the hotdog and peanut vendors than the players. One child was observed opening a peanut shell and finding inside two dark, shriveled nuts. When he placed those little beauties into his mouth, he quickly spit them out. An adult would realize the taste would be bad because they were rotten.

When Christians meet together they, too, may appear similar on the surface, but on the inside, some are hurting and rotting away. Often envy lies at the root of such rottenness.

It is a deadly toxin that poisons spiritual vitality.

Are there times when you go to church with a deep hurt, but wear the mask of joy?

EXPLAINING ENVY
(Genesis 30:1-16; Proverbs 14:30; Matthew 27:11-18; Acts 13:42-45; Romans 13:13; Galatians 5:26; James 3:14-16)

Do you agree with this definition? In what ways?

The Reader's Digest Great Encyclopedia Dictionary defines envy as a "feeling of resentment or discontent over another's superior attainments, endowments, or possessions." More simply stated, we would describe envy as resentment against another's success. Can envy really poison Christians? Unfortunately it can, and does. A believer is not immune to envy simply because he is a Christian.

Our heavenly Father knows that envy is a toxin, so in His love He warns us against it. He calls envy "the rottenness of the bones" (Proverbs 14:30). Sometimes we look at an unbeliever's success, and wonder why God lets him have it so good. Here we are, trying to please the Lord, yet the grass looks greener on the unbeliever's side of the fence. Sadly, if a Christian envies the sinner, he sins in doing so, for envy is sin.

Note the warning in Proverbs 3:31.

The Apostle Paul exhorted: "Let us walk honestly, as in the day; not in rioting and drunkenness, not in chambering and wantonness, not in strife and envying" (Romans 13:13). Did you notice the company that envy keeps? We abhor drunkenness and immorality, but if we envy, we keep the same company.

Notice the company envy keeps (Galatians 5:19-21).

It is not hard to find examples of envy in the Bible. The Bible is an honest book. It portrays man, as someone has stated, "warts and all." We can observe envy in Cain over the acceptance of his brother's offering. We can feel the envy of

Rachel because of Leah's ability to bear children. And we can sense among the children of Jacob the deep envy they felt toward the favorite son of the family, Joseph. These personal hurts and damaged relationships all resulted from the unchecked resentment of another's well-being.

In the New Testament two more examples of envy can be noted. When Jesus Christ was standing before the procurator, the Jewish leaders pressed Pilate for his death. Pilate wanted to free Christ, but he was afraid of the Jews. So he offered the crowd a choice between Jesus and Barabbas. He thought the people would choose Jesus, knowing that it was the chief priests and elders who wanted Him crucified. Pilate even understood the motive behind their behavior: "For he knew that for envy they had delivered him" (Matthew 27:18). The Jewish leaders crucified the Son of God because they allowed the poison of envy to possess them.

The Apostle Paul encountered the same resistance that our Lord experienced, and the reason for the opposition and persecution was, again, envy. After Paul and Barnabas preached in the synagogue at Antioch, some of the Jews, even some of the Gentile proselytes, believed in the Lord. And the following Sabbath nearly the whole city gathered to hear Paul and Barnabas' message from the Scriptures.

One would think that the religious leaders would have been thrilled that the people wanted to hear the Word of God. Rather, they stirred up the influential people of the city, and persecuted Paul and Barnabas, expelling them from their coast (Acts 13:50). Earlier in the account the reason is given why they behaved this way: "But

Take time to review these examples: Genesis 4:1-16; Genesis 30:1-16; Genesis 37:1-11 when the Jews saw the multitudes, they were filled with envy, and spake against those things which were spoken by Paul, contradicting and blaspheming" (Acts 13:45).

This poison of envy led the chief priests to crucify Christ, and the same deadly toxin led the Jews to persecute Paul. Their resentment over the crowds listening to the Word so poisoned them spiritually, that they committed the greatest of sins, blasphemy.

From the examples of envy in the Bible, and from our own experiences with envy, several harmful effects can be observed.

First, envy poisons the person who envies. Proverbs 14:30 states: "A sound heart is the life of the flesh: but envy the rottenness of the bones." We read in Job 5:2 that "wrath killeth the foolish man, and envy slayeth the silly one." Envy rots a person from within. It is the foolish, silly person who will let envy dry his spiritual vitality and slay his joy.

Second, envy has a toxic effect on the Body of Christ. The writer of Proverbs asks the question: "Who is able to stand before envy?" (Proverbs 27:4). Its damage to relationships is obvious. James expressed the disorderly and hurtful effect of this sin when he warned: "But if ye have bitter envying and strife in your hearts, glory not, and lie not against the truth. This wisdom descendeth not from above, but is earthly, sensual, devilish. For where envying and strife is, there is confusion and every evil work" (James 3:14-16).

Third, envy has an adverse effect upon the lost. Nonbelievers are to see our good deeds and, as a result, glorify our Father (Matthew 5:16). They are to see a radiant, godly lifestyle, and therefore ask

> Unconfessed sin is like a snowball growing larger as it rolls down a hillside.

> Too often our lives are lived in reaction to others, rather than in following the Holy Spirit.

25

the reason for our hope (I Peter 3:15). They are to observe love and genuine caring among Christians and conclude that it is because we are followers of Christ (John 13:35). Instead, when they see discontent and discord of envy, they conclude: "These people really aren't any different from me; they have nothing I need."

Fourth, envy insults God, for it assaults His character by challenging His sovereignty. Who dares question what God chooses to do or permits in His world? Paul explains: "Nay but, O man, who art thou that repliest against God? Shall the thing formed say to the thing that formed it, Why hast thou made me thus? Hath not the potter power over the clay, of the same lump to make one vessel unto honour, and the other unto dishonour?" (Romans 9:20,21).

When a Christian envies, he is insulting God, challenging God's choice in allowing another to prosper, be successful, or have some advantages. God's Word tells us that "all things work together for good to them that love God, to them who are the called according to his purpose" (Romans 8:28). The individual who feels "resentment or discontent over another's superior attainments, endowments or possessions," however, is not accepting what the Potter has allowed. The discontent and unthankfulness rots away the believer's inner joy, but even worse it insults God.

EXTINGUISHING ENVY
(Psalm 115:1-3; I Thessalonians 5:15-19)

Many young children first earn a little spending money by doing chores around their house. In the spring some receive the standard "penny a weed" (if root intact) to pull those eyesores from the lawn. At first, it is not unlikely to see children go after the big weeds, because they are so noticeable. They soon find out, however, that the tall weeds have deeper roots, and are more difficult to remove completely. It is easier to pull the smaller weeds before they root deeply in the lawn. Similarly, it is easier for us to fight envy on an ongoing basis—every time it begins to grow in our lives. Two things will help us overcome the poison of envy.

First we need to have a healthy view of the sovereignty of God. The Psalmist reminds believers: "But our God is in the heavens: he hath done whatsoever he hath pleased" (Psalm 115:3). No one prospers outside God's knowledge; nor does anyone get cancer outside His sovereignty. This is not saying that God initiates every event in a person's life. Often we reap the consequences of choices; sometimes Satan is back to his old "sifting" tricks; at other times we experience the problems inherent in a sin-cursed world. Nevertheless, even in these circumstances God is sovereign. He could directly intervene in a situation, and sometimes does, but His greatest concern is that, through the good and bad of life, we grow in Christlike character.

Every person will give an account of the stewardship God has entrusted to him (Matthew 25:14f). Whether our stewardship is great or small, we trust His wise choice and respond as faithful servants. We also trust the fairness of God as He distributes to others, for we know that they too will be judged according to their advantages.

The greater our understanding of the sover-

> Can you think of a situation that you allowed to go unchecked, and then later it was harder to correct?

> "Whatsoever the Lord pleased, that he did in heaven, and in earth, in the seas, and all deep places" (Psalm 135:6).

> The believer will not be judged for salvation, but for his stewardship. See II Corinthians 5:10.

27

eignty of God, the easier it will be for us to guard against envy. God makes His sovereign choices in harmony with His omniscience, His love, His mercy and His wisdom. What He brings into each life is His concern, not what He allows in another's life.

The second step in fighting envy is to cultivate a thankful attitude. Replace envy with thanksgiving. Discontentment and resentment are poisons; praise and thanksgiving are healing medicines.

"If you think, you'll thank."

On a radio program a psychiatrist was being interviewed on the subject of mental health. He stated that although he did not personally believe in God, he encouraged his patients to practice thanking God daily for things in their lives. He stated that this simple practice proved better than any other form of therapy to help people out of depression.

This counselor's prescription was not new; actually, it was given centuries ago. Paul advised: "Rejoice evermore. Pray without ceasing. In every thing give thanks: for this is the will of God in Christ Jesus concerning you" (I Thessalonians 5:16-18). Why is this the will of God? Because God is concerned for our well-being, and He knows that trust and acceptance bring peace and joy.

God is working to bring things together for the good of each Christian. Sometimes we do not understand how a particular piece of the puzzle fits into our lives, but God takes all the pieces and works them together to make us into the likeness of his dear Son.

The "good" in Romans 8:28 is defined in verse 29: "conformed to the image of his Son."

Knowing that it is because of His love, wisdom, and grace that God allows things to enter our lives, we can sincerely express appreciation for

28

what is His will. Being thankful for what the Lord allows in our lives and for what He permits in the lives of others extinguishes both the resentment over their blessings and the covetous desire to have what they have.

NOW TEST YOUR KNOWLEDGE

Answer true or false:

1. Envy is my problem; it doesn't affect others.
2. Rachel's envy strengthened her relationship with Jacob.
3. Joseph's brothers had good reasons for being envious of him.
4. Envy is an expression of ingratitude to God for my situation.
5. Envy challenges the sovereignty of God.
6. Envy was the motive behind the crucifixion of Jesus.
7. Envy is a barrier to gospel witness.

Fill in the Blank:

8. "A sound heart is life to the flesh: but envy the _____ of _____ _____."
9. "... who is able to _____ before _____?"
10. "For where envy and strife is, there is _____ _____ and every _____ _____."

FOOD FOR THOUGHT

"Envy shoots at others and wounds herself."
—Anonymous

4

I CAN'T KICK THE HABIT:
THE TOXIN OF BAD HABITS
I CORINTHIANS 6:9-12; 10:1-15; LUKE 11:24-26;
EPHESIANS 4:17-32

EVERY DAY WITH THE WORD

Monday	Recognizing	I Corinthians 10:1-15
Tuesday	Rethinking	Psalm 42:5-11
Wednesday	Replacing	Luke 11:24-26
Thursday	Retraining	Ephesians 4:17-32
Friday	Reckoning	I Corinthians 6:9-12
Saturday	Resisting	Genesis 39
Sunday	Renewing	Romans 12:1-9

Learn by Heart:
"All things are lawful unto me, but all things are not expedient: all things are lawful for me, but I will not be brought under the power of any" (I Corinthians 6:12).

Whether we realize it or not, we are creatures of habit. We usually shop at the same stores, travel the same highways, and even eat the same types of food. It is very likely that if you wore a shirt or blouse today, you buttoned it in a predictable pattern. Some move from the top down; some move from the bottom up; and others begin with the third button from the top, move to the bottom, and conclude with the top two buttons. Whether it is the way we brush our teeth, the manner in which we read the newspaper, or the way we clean house, our repetition proves we are—

As you begin this chapter, ask the Holy Spirit to identify any sins or practices in your life that are not under your control.

CREATURES OF HABIT
(I Corinthians 10:1-15; Luke 11:24-26)

Everyone has habits. Habit formation is not wrong in itself. In fact, our daily living is enhanced by our patterned responses. For example, when a person first begins to drive a car the actions of starting the engine, moving the gear shift, and operating the wheel and pedals consume so much of his mental energy that the experience is emotionally draining. After a few years of driving, however, he is struck by the realization that he drives from work to home without even remembering being in the car, traveling on the expressway, or parking the car in the garage.

Read one or two dictionary definitions of "habit."

A habit is a behavior that is practiced so often that it becomes an automatic response. Being creatures of habit is not our problem. Rather, it is the type of behavior we find ourselves enslaved to that alarms us. Habits that are God-honoring produce spiritual growth; habits that are worldly slowly poison us. The Scripture reminds us: "And be not conformed to this world: but be ye transformed by the renewing of your mind, that ye may prove what is that good, and acceptable, and perfect, will of God" (Romans 12:2). We do not need to be victims of harmful habits. We can be proactive in the choice of habits we desire for our lives.

While Christians may realize that complaining, temper, lust, overeating, and worry are sins, many have never stopped to realize the seriousness of these sins. When a sin is repeated so frequently that it develops into a habit, the sinful practice becomes idolatry. In the wilderness Israel put their desire for immorality and pleasure-seeking ahead of God. And Israel was punished for doing so. Consequently we are warned: "Now these things were our examples, to the intent that we should not lust after evil things, as they also

The adversary wants us to suppress this thought. He'd rather we sin and then think it really doesn't affect our relationship with God.

31

lusted! Neither be ye idolaters, as were some of them . . . " (I Corinthians 10:6,7a).

When a person repeatedly yields to a temptation, it becomes a habit and an idol. Notice how Paul relates temptation and idolatry. "There hath no temptation taken you but such as is common to man: but God is faithful, who will not suffer you to be tempted above that ye are able; but will with the temptation also make a way to escape, that ye may be able to bear it. Wherefore, my dearly beloved, flee from idolatry" (I Corinthians 10:13,14).

We are not victims of circumstance. If indulging in a sinful practice ingrains that practice in us, conversely, through the power of the Holy Spirit, that habit can be reversed.

If a person eliminates a sinful behavior without establishing a new healthy behavior in its place he will create an emptiness in his life. Notice how Jesus communicated this truth. He said: "When the unclean spirit is gone out of a man, he walketh through dry places, seeking rest; and finding none, he saith, I will return unto my house whence I came out. And when he cometh, he findeth it swept and garnished. Then goeth he and taketh to him seven other spirits more wicked than himself; and they enter in, and dwell there: and the last state of the man is worse than the first" (Luke 11:24-26). Those who are enslaved to a sinful habit can identify with the words of Christ, that their current situation is even more serious.

While some Christians might be tempted to claim they just can't help themselves, very few would suggest that God is powerless to help them. While theologically they attest to the omnipotence of the Holy Spirit within them, their lives reveal a

> It is sad to realize that Christians in your class, or at your church, wrestle with the same temptations, but few acknowledge such or team together for support.

> Christ's story also illustrates the futility of mere human effort against spiritual forces.

failure to appropriate that power. Some may honestly confess that they love their sinful indulgence more than they do the will of God. Some may be fooled by the adversary into believing that God doesn't mind if they keep a few old-nature habits. Some can identify with Paul, that they feel wretched over some sinful practice and desire spiritual victory.

It would be easier for us if God removed Satan's presence from the world and eradicated our sin nature. It would be nice if we could just take an "anti-lust pill" or "anti-complaining pill" to eliminate our sinful habits, but this is not God's desire. God does not abhor testings and trials, as we do. In fact, they are part of His plan for measuring our true love for Him and for helping us mature in Him.

While we are creatures of habit, our loving heavenly Father desires that we be—

CHILDREN OF HOLINESS
(I Corinthians 6:9-12; Ephesians 4:17-32)

The Apostle Paul was not a super saint because he had a monopoly on the Holy Spirit. He was a spiritual giant because the Holy Spirit had a monopoly on him. Paul's desire was that his life be maximized for God's use. He did not want to be held down by any weight; he wanted to be free from anything that would hold him back.

Paul guarded his life against undesirable habits, even those which some would call "the gray areas." He confessed: "All things are lawful unto me, but all things are not expedient: all things are lawful for me, but I will not be brought under the power of any" (I Corinthians 6:12).

Many Christians have the same aspirations as Paul, but they are defeated by enslaving habits. Just as a surgeon removes a cancer, so they have tried to cut out a particular sin that easily overcomes them. Unfortunately, many find that after a period of time, they fall back into their old habit. At that point the adversary recognizes that he has them on the ropes, and he plants the thought in their minds: "I can't help myself; this is just the way I am."

See Hebrews 12:1,2.

Once we understand the nature of sinful habits, that they are idols and need not master us, we can embark on the exciting adventure of gaining victory over them. Each day we can look forward to becoming more successful in worshiping God rather than bowing down to a bad habit. The key is to replace a bad habit with a good one.

This principle of replacement is explained by Paul in his letter to the church at Ephesus. He wrote: "That ye put off concerning the former conversation the old man, which is corrupt according to the deceitful lusts; And be renewed in the spirit of your mind; And that ye put on the new man, which after God is created in righteousness and true holiness" (Ephesians 4:22-24). Notice that Paul is speaking of behaviors, not feelings. Rather than following the leading of our feelings, we are to let our renewed thinking, our mind, reshape our will.

The principle can also be called "retraining."

Notice in Psalm 42 how David used his mind to analyze and challenge the validity of his feelings.

God has provided us with a Manual that not only describes healthy behaviors but also provides examples of these behaviors in the lives of godly people. The Scriptures show us how not to behave and how to behave. As we meditate upon the Word, our mind is programmed with God's viewpoint. The Holy Spirit then reminds us of those words at critical moments. We are advised in Proverbs: "For as he thinketh in his heart, so is he" (23:7). Overcoming an enslaving habit begins by replacing worldly thinking and behavior with godly thinking and behavior. In addition to the principle of replacing, the Christian must also be involved in resisting.

The promise of I Corinthians 10:13 is that God will not allow His children to be tested beyond their resistance. God also affirmed that He will provide a means of victory with every temptation. One strategy for victory studied previously is to use the Scripture in standing firm against the adversary. Just as Jesus was tempted three times by the devil, and refuted his false values with the truth of Scripture, so too, a believer can stand firm in the Scriptures.

A second means of escape that is available to the believer is to remove himself from a temptation. For someone who struggles with lust, watching a sensuous program on television or at a theater is like playing with dynamite. God's way of escape can be to not even begin to watch that kind of program. In the words of Paul: "Put ye on the Lord Jesus, and make not provision for the flesh, to fulfil the lusts thereof" (Romans 13:14).

Instead of being enslaved to sinful habits, believers can be children of holiness by replacing and resisting sinful temptations. Furthermore, a way has been provided for getting us back on track when we fall. That way is the renewing of our spiritual commitment.

Rather than letting Satan keep him from standing again, the believer needs to confess his sin (I John 1:9) and recommit his life to God. The admonition to the Christians at Rome, is just as

The armor for spiritual warfare given in Ephesians 6:10-18 leads to victory even over the most stubborn habits.

Matthew 4:10.

35

crucial to us today: "That ye present your bodies a living sacrifice, holy, acceptable unto God, which is your reasonable service" (Romans 12:1).

Habit formation is good. We can use this natural process of God for victory in our Christian lives. For many who are enslaved by habits that dishonor God, the possibility of victory is assured. Agreeing with God that sinful habits are idolatry will put us on the right course of recovery. The principles of replacing, resisting and renewing can be used daily in reversing sinful habits.

Remember:
"...we are more than conquerors through him that loved us"
(Romans 8:37).

NOW TEST YOUR KNOWLEDGE

Answer true or false:

1. A sinful habit is an idol.
2. All temptations can be resisted.
3. No one has faced the same temptation that I have faced.
4. Satan gave up tempting Jesus.
5. Resisting sin might involve avoiding potentially sinful situations.

Match the following:

6. The importance of reckoning.   A. Romans 12:1
7. The principle of replacing.   B. I Corinthians 6:12
8. An example of resisting.   C. I John 1:9
9. The necessity of confessing.   D. Genesis 39:10
10. The need for renewing.   E. Ephesians 4:22-24

FOOD FOR THOUGHT

"Sow an act, and you reap a habit; sow a habit, and you reap a character; sow a character, and you reap a destiny."
—G. D. Boardman

5

GRIPE, GRIPE, GRIPE:
THE TOXIN OF COMPLAINING
NUMBERS 11; 12; PHILIPPIANS 4:6,7; I PETER 5:6-11;
I JOHN 1:9

EVERY DAY WITH THE WORD

Monday	Complaint #1	Numbers 11:1-3
Tuesday	Complaint #2	Numbers 11:4-10,31-35
Wednesday	Complaint #3	Numbers 11:10-30
Thursday	Complaint #4	Numbers 12
Friday	Contentment and confession	Philippians 4:11-16; I John 1
Saturday	Praise	Psalm 89:1-7
Sunday	Sincere concerns	I Peter 5:6-11

Think about the communication in your home or at work this past week. Was complaining present? How did it affect relationships?

In one family we hear: "Gripe, gripe, gripe; that's all you ever do!" In another family we hear: "If you can't say anything positive, don't say anything at all!" In a third home the accusation is made: "All you ever do is complain!"

How does God respond to complaining? Is it always wrong to complain? In the Old Testament book of Numbers, God has recorded four case studies of complaining. Noting how God responds to those complaints can help us overcome the poison of complaining.

COMPLAINING: OLD TESTAMENT STYLE
(Numbers 11; 12)

Numbers records the wilderness wanderings. Exodus records the deliverance of God's people from Egypt and their receiving of the law. In

Numbers the Hebrews are moving from Sinai toward the Promised Land. The events in Numbers show the importance of doing the Lord's work the Lord's way. Because the Hebrews feared the occupants of Canaan, they refused to take possession of their inheritance when they reached Canaan's border. And, because of that decision which showed a lack of trust in God, the entire adult generation, with the exception of Joshua and Caleb, died in the wilderness.

Throughout Israel's wanderings God was teaching them lessons on faith. Over and over again He had remarkably provided for His children. By the time they reached Kadesh-Barnea, at Canaan's border, they should have looked at God's track record, and realized that He would give them the land. Unfortunately, they repeatedly failed to put their trust in God. Fixing their eyes on their own problems, they complained about their hardships and wanderings. Their complaints were more than just expressions of discontentment. They were assaults on the character of God.

Four complaints are registered in Numbers 11 and 12. The first is the Israelites' complaint. Numbers 11:1-3 reveals: "And when the people complained, it displeased the Lord: and the Lord heard it; and his anger was kindled; and the fire of the Lord burnt among them, and consumed them that were in the uttermost parts of the camp. And the people cried unto Moses; and when Moses prayed unto the Lord, the fire was quenched. And he called the name of the place Taberah: because the fire of the Lord burnt among them."

Although the text is not specific on the nature of this complaint, it appears from the preceding

To get the overall impact of how serious complaining was in the camp of Israel, read Numbers 11 and 12 at one sitting.

Several of the previous complaints are recorded in the book of Exodus.

38

chapters that the people were tired of their wilderness wanderings. Yes, the desert was hot and dusty. Yes, they did not have their homes in Egypt, but neither did they have their taskmasters and abusive treatment. So quickly they had forgotten the intensity of their oppression that led them to call out to God for deliverance.

Instead of looking forward to "the land flowing with milk and honey," they complained. Whether the complaints were internal or voiced, whether murmurings among small groups or major protests, the Lord heard their accusations, and they "displeased the Lord."

Because of their selfish complaints, God judged the people. He sent fire to burn the perimeter of the camp as a sign of His displeasure. Although it is not certain from the text that people were slain in the fire, it is possible that some of the rabble were consumed.

A second case of complaining was, again, the Israelites. Not long after God's visible judgment, the people began to express their preference for greener looking grass on Egypt's side of the fence. Their specific gripe focused on the absence of the kinds of food they lacked. The Biblical account states: "And the mixt multitude that was among them fell a lusting: and the children of Israel also wept again, and said, Who shall give us flesh to eat? We remember the fish, which we did eat in Egypt freely; the cucumbers, and the melons, and the leeks, and the onions and the garlick: But now our soul is dried away: there is nothing at all, beside this manna, before our eyes" (Numbers 11:4-6).

What other nation had nutritious food delivered fresh daily? What other people were able to

The words "them that were" in verse 1 are not in the Hebrew. The KJV italicizes them to show they are the translator's clarifying interpretation.

Their complaint seems reality-based in that they did not have these foods. However, they did not *need* these foods, so their complaint was selfish.

39

partake of as much food as they wanted, without preparation or cleanup? God supernaturally provided manna for His people, but they complained because of this restrictive diet.

Notice the intensity of their bitterness. The people were "weeping" (throughout their families), and they were complaining to one another ("Who shall give us flesh to eat?"). Even Moses was aware of their discontent, for he "heard the people weep throughout their families, every man in the door of his tent" (verse 10).

Again, the Lord's response to their self-pity and complaining was judgment. He was angered by their lack of appreciation, and in an attempt to illustrate the seriousness of their lack of trust, He disciplined them.

When Moses brought the people's complaint to the Lord, the Lord said He would give them meat until they were sick of it. Verses 18 to 20 reveal: "And say thou unto the people, Sanctify yourselves against tomorrow, and ye shall eat flesh: for ye have wept in the ears of the Lord, saying, Who shall give us flesh to eat? for it was well with us in Egypt: therefore the Lord will give you flesh, and ye shall eat. Ye shall not eat one day, nor two days, nor five days, neither ten days, nor twenty days; But even a whole month, until it comes out at your nostrils, and it be loathsome unto you: because that ye have despised the Lord which is among you, and have wept before him, saying, "Why came we forth out of Egypt?"

The reason God was displeased is understandable. Israel's complaining about their situation meant they were complaining about the Lord of their situation. God, knowing their hearts, identified their sin: "Ye have despised the Lord which is

Their discontent spread from self, to family members, to the community.

God may choose to discipline our selfishness by sometimes giving us what we ask, even if it is not in our best interest.

The people may not have been aware that their complaining was despising the Lord. Do we realize that our discontent is a form of despising God?

among you" (verse 20).

The complaining was not done in privacy. Being discontent in spirit would have been bad enough, but Israel grumbled in public, making this toxin even more poisonous. God's judgment fell among the people while they were gorging themselves with His provision of quail. Verses 33,34 tell us: "And while the flesh was yet between their teeth, ere it was chewed, the wrath of the Lord was kindled against the people, and the Lord smote the people with a very great plague. And he called the name of that place Kibroth-hattaavah: because there they buried the people that lusted." The ringleaders of the rebellion were especially noted by God, and were disciplined as an example to the rest of the people.

Moses provides a third example of complaining. In the middle of the account of the people's complaining about the lack of meat, Moses complained about how hard it was to be Israel's leader. Once again, the children of Israel had unloaded on Moses, and he felt the double pressure of representing them before God and God before them. Moses lamented to the Lord, "Wherefore hast thou afflicted thy servant? and wherefore have I not found favour in thy sight, that thou layest the burden of all this people upon me? Have I conceived all this people? have I begotten them, that thou shouldest say unto me, Carry them in thy bosom, as a nursing father beareth the sucking child, unto the land which thou swarest unto their fathers? Whence should I have flesh to give unto all this people? for they weep unto me, saying, Give us flesh, that we may eat. I am not able to bear all this people alone, because it is too heavy for me" (verses 11-14).

God warns against all personal sin, but especially against leading others into sin. See for example Matthew 18:6.

Notice the depth of Moses' discouragement, even to the point of wishing God would take his life (Numbers 11:15).

Moses was overwhelmed with his heavy leadership responsibility, and he took his sincere complaint to the Lord. Notice that God did not respond to Moses with judgment. Rather, He answered Moses' serious need by saying He would spiritually equip the seventy elders of Israel to help him with his task (verses 16,17). God provided Moses with help for carrying the burden of the people, and He also gave him an answer for the people in response to their complaint.

The fourth example of complaining is the accusation brought by Miriam and Aaron in Numbers 12. "And Miriam and Aaron spake against Moses because of the Ethiopian woman whom he had married: for he had married an Ethiopian woman. And they said, hath the Lord indeed spoken only by Moses? hath he not spoken also by us? And the Lord heard it" (12:1,2). Their initial complaint centered on the type of woman Moses married. However, that was not what bothered them most. The real issue was one of authority and leadership. They didn't like Moses calling all the shots. Their question, "Hath the Lord indeed spoken *only* by Moses?" reveals envy as the motivation underlying their complaint.

> The Lord always hears our complaints; they too are insults to His gracious provision in our lives.

God's response to the selfish complaint was one of judgment. "And the anger of the Lord was kindled against them; and he departed. And the cloud departed from off the tabernacle; and, behold, Miriam became leprous, white as snow: and Aaron looked upon Miriam, and, behold, she was leprous" (verses 9,10). God's judgment was that Miriam became leprous. She would have to be put outside the camp. Even though Aaron was a priest, he was helpless to change her condition.

> Leprosy was a skin disease that required isolation of the afflicted.

What application can believers make from these examples of complaining? A comparison of the four complaints provides insight into—

COMPLAINING: 20TH CENTURY STYLE
(I John 1:9; I Peter 5:6-11)

A careful analysis of the four examples of complaining recorded in Numbers 11 and 12 reveals that God responded differently to the complaints. Moses had a sincere complaint and took it to God, while the people had selfish complaints and shared them with each other. The Israelites were accusing and slandering God and Moses. They were challenging God's sovereignty and His love. The people were not grateful for God's supernatural provision; nor were Miriam and Aaron grateful for their special position. God judged these people for their selfish complaints.

Just as a parent wants his child to share what is troubling him, so too, even those things which cause discontent within us should be brought to our heavenly Father in prayer.

Even though Moses wasn't free from self-pity, his concern was not just for himself. He had a sincere love for both God and the Israelites. Moses didn't complain to the seventy elders about his burden, or complain to them that God was unfair. He took his complaint directly to God, and God responded by meeting Moses' need.

Two principles leap from these pages of ancient history. First, *selfish complaints should be brought to God for confession.* Among the seven things listed in Proverbs 6:16-19 as detestable to God is: "he that soweth discord among brethren" (verse 19). There is no legitimacy in the Christian life for believers to voice displeasure with their situation. Rather, they should bring all their concerns to God. Paul counsels: "Be careful for nothing; but in every thing by prayer and supplication with thanksgiving let your requests be made known

Continue further in Philippians 4, noting the apostle's attitude in verses 11-16.

43

unto God" (Philippians 4:6).

Recall the promise of I John 1:9, that, "if we confess our sins, he is faithful and just to forgive us our sins, and to cleanse us from all unrighteousness." This promise certainly applies to the toxin of complaining. When we find ourselves discontent and griping over self-centered issues, we need to bring those concerns to the Lord in confession.

The second principle we gain from our study of the four cases of complaining in Numbers 11 and 12 is this: *We should bring sincere complaints to God for His counsel.* An old hymn pleads: "Have we trials and temptations? Is there trouble anywhere? We should never be discouraged, Take it to the Lord in prayer. Can we find a friend so faithful, Who will all our sorrows share? Jesus knows our every weakness, take it to the Lord in prayer." The adversary uses discontent to devour Christians. Instead of being discontent, we can heed the invitation: "Casting all your care upon him; for he careth for you" (see I Peter 5:7).

If a deadly toxin enters a person's blood stream, and he refuses to believe that it will hurt him, he will die. If we believe our self-centered complaints are legitimate, or only call them personal concerns, and refuse to recognize that our complaining is sinful, we will lose our spiritual vitality. The toxin will have a deadening effect on us.

God has recorded these examples of complaining so that we would respond to Him in greater depth of trust. We can be victors, triumphing over even a grumbling spirit. We can identify with the psalmist who proclaimed: "With my mouth will I make known thy faithfulness to all generations" (Psalm 89:1).

If you own a hymnal, take a moment to read the lyrics of "What A Friend We Have In Jesus."

If you own a hymnal, take a moment to read the lyrics of "What A Friend We Have In Jesus."

We were created to be people of praise. Take a moment just now to praise the Lord. Also commit anew your mouth to Him, that your speech this week would be to the praise of His glory. See Psalm 89:1-7.

NOW TEST YOUR KNOWLEDGE

Fill in the blanks:

1. "Casting_____ _____ _____ upon him; for he careth for you."
2. "And when the people complained, it _____ the Lord; and the Lord heard it; and his anger was kindled."
3. "Be_____ for_____; but in every thing by prayer and supplication with thanksgiving let your requests be made known unto God."
4. "I will _____ of the mercies of the Lord forever: with my _____ will I make known thy faithfulness to all generations."

Answer true or false:

5. Complaining hurts me, my relationships with others, and my relationship with God.
6. Complaining is often an overflow from a self-centered attitude.
7. I should keep my complaints to myself.
8. Some complaints reflect a sincere problem.
9. Selfish complaints and sincere complaints should both be brought to the Lord.
10. We should seek God's counsel for both selfish and sincere complaints.

FOOD FOR THOUGHT

"The usual fortune of complaint is to excite contempt more than pity."
—Samuel Johnson

6

I AM THE GREATEST:
THE TOXIN OF PRIDE
PROVERBS 11:2; 16:5,18; 29:23; ISAIAH 14:12-17; DANIEL
3:1-5; 4:17-37; 5:20,21; LUKE 18:9-14; PHILIPPIANS 2:1-11

EVERY DAY WITH THE WORD

Monday	Pride's character	Isaiah 14:12-17
Tuesday	Pride's cost	Luke 18:9-14
Wednesday	Pride's condemnation	Daniel 4:17-37
Thursday	Pride's consequences	Proverbs 11:2; 16:5,18; 29:23
Friday	Pride's confrontation	I Peter 5:1-6
Saturday	Pride's corrective	Ephesians 4:1-6
Sunday	Pride's cure	Philippians 2:1-11

Learn by Heart: "Humble yourselves therefore under the mighty hand of God, that he may exalt you in due time" (I Peter 5:6).

While Christians can rejoice that they are "fearfully and wonderfully made" (Psalm 139:14), they must have a proper appraisal of themselves lest they fall victims to the adversary's toxin of pride. How can we distinguish between a healthy self-concept and an unhealthy exaltation?

DESCRIBING PRIDE
(Isaiah 14:12-17; Luke 18:9-14)

Proverbs 6:6-19 lists seven things that are an abomination to God. At the head of the list is "a proud look." The Bible's warning that the Lord hates these things should impact us the same way a poison warning label on a bottle cautions us. Pride is a toxin because it kills our spiritual vitality.

Pride is the characteristic of having too high an

opinion of one's own importance. It is an attitude of superiority which may surface in behavior such as boasting, swaggering, or snobbishness. Some who have a high opinion of themselves will go to the opposite extreme. They will put themselves down with comments such as, "Oh, I'm not very good," or "I really don't think I can do that." A person who is gifted and able, yet keeps running himself down, is drawing as much attention to himself as the person who is boastful. This type of false humility seeks to elicit responses from others that say, "Oh, you really are good," or "I really think you can do it." False humility is really pride.

A person may not be aware that his self-abasement is really a form of pride.

If any Bible personality had a basis for spiritual pride, it would have been the Apostle Paul. From persecutor of the church to proclaimer of the truth, Paul had seen a remarkable change in his life. Being raised to the position of "Apostle to the Gentiles" would have been difficult for most people to handle with humility. Yet Paul never forgot the seriousness of his sin, the pit from which he had been dug. That realization along with his "thorn in the flesh" gave him a balanced appraisal of himself.

Paul described his spiritual heritage and discipline in Philippians 3:4-6. Yet he boasted only in the righteousness which comes by faith. See verses 7-10.

The word balance is important. Paul wrote to believers so that they would have a healthy understanding of who they were, would appreciate their relationship with other believers, and would grow in their relationship with God. He admonished the Romans: "For I say, through the grace given unto me, to every man that is among you, not to think of himself more highly than he ought to think; but to think soberly, according as God hath dealt to every man the measure of faith" (Romans 12:3).

Paul realized that everything he had was due to grace. He informed the Romans that believers are predestined, called, justified and glorified. He explained that the Holy Spirit intercedes for us, that God works for our good in all circumstances, and that nothing can separate us from God's love. As believers, we should have a good self-image; however, Paul said we need to guard against thinking "more highly" of ourselves than we should.

Romans 8:26-39

Pride is an inordinate opinion of our own merit or worth. The adversary likes to tempt us to be proud because pride poisons us; and, like so many sins, pride insults God. Because of his pride, Satan was removed from his high angelic status. Also, because of his pride Nebuchadnezzar, King of Babylon, was humiliated. Believers wrestle against "principalities, against powers, against the rulers of the darkness of this world, against spiritual wickedness in high places," according to Ephesians 6:12. While human beings govern the nations, demons try to influence their governing. For example, the prince of Persia withstood the Archangel Michael for twenty days. Behind the person who ruled Persia, was a demon who was assigned to that kingdom.

See Daniel 10:13.

The book of Isaiah includes a description of a ruler's pride. The message is addressed to the King of Babylon, but also to Satan, who was behind his rule. Pride characterized the attitude of both the King of Babylon and of Satan. Isaiah 14:12-14 reads: "How art thou fallen from heaven, O Lucifer, son of the morning! how art thou cut down to the ground, which didst weaken the nations! For thou hast said in thine heart, I will

When we say "I" too frequently, we are thinking of others too infrequently.

ascend into heaven, I will exalt my throne above the stars of God: I will sit also upon the mount of the congregation, in the sides of the north: I will ascend above the heights of the clouds; I will be like the most High."

Five times the pronoun "I" appears in Isaiah 14:12-14. There would be nothing inherently wrong with the King of Babylon recognizing his prominent position; nor would there be anything wrong with Satan appreciating the fact that he was created as the highest of angels. They were guilty of sin because they weren't content to be less than God Himself. Unhappy with his created status, Satan dared believe that he could "be like the most High." Forgetting the God of Daniel, Nebuchadnezzar thought he was the greatest person in Babylon.

The Lord Jesus warned about pride. In one of His parables, He contrasted the pride of a Pharisee with the humility of a publican. The underlying cause of the Pharisee's pride is revealed by these words: "And he spake this parable unto certain which trusted in themselves that they were righteous, and despised others" (Luke 18:9). What was behind the Pharisee's snobbish attitude? It was the fact that he believed he was self-righteous. He was a humanist in the sense that he felt completely adequate without God.

You can read the parable of the Pharisee and the publican in Luke 18:9-14.

Satan thought he could be like God, Nebuchadnezzar thought he was the greatest, and the Pharisee had an inordinate opinion about himself. All these failed to appreciate and acknowledge that they owed everything to God. God allowed them to have their special positions, gifts and abilities.

DEFEATING PRIDE
(Proverbs 11:2; 16:5,18; 29:23; Daniel 3:1-5; 4:17-37; 5:20,21; Philippians 2:1-11)

The deadliness of the toxin of pride is noted from Satan's fall and Jesus' teaching. The prophecy in Isaiah 14 continues with these words: "Yet thou shalt be brought down to hell, to the sides of the pit" (verse 15). Similarly, in the parable of the Pharisee and the publican, Jesus stated: "I tell you, this man [the publican] went down to his house justified rather than the other [the Pharisee]: for everyone that exalteth himself shall be abased; and he that humbleth himself shall be exalted" (Luke 18:14). God hates pride. It is an abomination to Him. He will judge it.

God opposes the proud for three reasons. First, *pride is self-destructive*. Several proverbs teach this. "When pride cometh, then cometh shame: but with the lowly is wisdom" (Proverbs 11:2). "Pride goeth before destruction, and a haughty spirit before a fall" (Proverbs 16:18). "A man's pride shall bring him low: but honour shall uphold the humble in spirit" (Proverbs 29:23).

King Nebuchadnezzar of Babylon is a clear example of how pride led to self-destruction. Isaiah prophesied his downfall, and the book of Daniel reveals his boastful attitude. Not only had Nebuchadnezzar made an image of gold (very likely of himself) that was to be worshiped, but he also looked at the great empire of Babylon and commended himself for his great accomplishments. Daniel 5:20,21 reveals: "But when his heart was lifted up, and his mind hardened in pride, he was deposed from his kingly throne, and

God does not keep people from fellowship with Him or from Heaven. People keep themselves from God because of their pride and self-righteousness.

Nebuchadnezzar did accomplish much, and Babylon was a beautiful city, but

50

the king failed to acknowledge that God allowed him his position.

they took his glory from him: And he was driven from the sons of men; and his heart was made like the beasts, and his dwelling was with the wild asses: they fed him with grass like oxen, and his body was wet with the dew of heaven; till he knew that the most high God ruled in the kingdom of men, and that he appointeth over it whomsoever he will." God judges pride because pride is self-destructive.

Second, *pride is condemned by God because it poisons others.* A person who is wrapped up in himself does not have time to think of the needs of others. This contradicts God's purpose for His people. When God saves a person, it is not only for the individual's well-being, but also for the good of others. God has chosen to use human instruments to make His love known to others. A proud, self-centered person sees only himself as important, so he doesn't care enough about others to share God's love with them. The Apostle Paul warned that we are not to think too highly of ourselves (Romans 12:3). And he encouraged us to recognize our inter-dependence in Christ. He wrote: "For as we have many members in one body, and all members have not the same office: So we, being many, are one body in Christ, and every one members one of another" (verses 4,5). Pride is destructive to interpersonal relationships and should, therefore, be abhorred.

The second commandment is to love your neighbor as yourself (Mark 12:31).

See also I Corinthians 12:13-27.

Third, God condemns pride because *it challenges God's sovereignty.* God alone is sovereign; He decrees and permits things to happen in His creation. Pride says: "I am the creator of my own life," or "I am the reason for my success." A proud person fails to realize that God has given him his I.Q., has allowed him to be born in a certain nation, to certain parents, with certain benefits and physical features.

If anyone had worth, importance, merit or superiority to boast of, it was the Lord Jesus Christ, the eternal Son of the Father, the Firstborn of all creation, the First and the Last, the King of kings and Lord of lords. Yet, throughout His earthly life, He demonstrated humility in His speech, behavior, and attitudes. Even when He spoke of His pre-existence and oneness with the Father, He did so with reserve, and to instruct rather than to boast.

If a Christian is to have an honest appraisal of himself, live in harmony with others, and honor God as Lord of his life, he must emulate the humility of Christ. Believers need to draw upon God's grace, for "God resisteth the proud, but giveth grace unto the humble" (James 4:6).

We are instructed in Ephesians 4:22-32 to put off the old man and to put on the new man; to put off the deeds of the flesh and to put on the fruit of the Spirit. If we try to purge pride from our lives without replacing the vacuum with humility and other-centeredness, we will not be delivered from this attack of Satan.

In every aspect of the Christian life we are to fix our eyes upon Christ. Paul urged the Philippians: "Let this mind be in you, which was also in Christ Jesus: Who being in the form of God, thought it not robbery to be equal with God: But made himself of no reputation, and took upon him the form of a servant, and was made in the likeness of men: And being found in fashion as a man, he humbled himself, and became obedient unto death, even the death on a cross" (Philippians 2:5-8). Jesus is our example of victory. His worth was

"Count your many blessings, name them one by one, and it will surprise you what the *Lord* has done!"

Some make it a habit to read the Gospels each year. That practice keeps the example of Jesus ever before them.

See Hebrews 12:2.

never in question at the incarnation. Even as He took on full humanity, He remained fully God. While He gave up the voluntary use of His attributes, nevertheless He was the eternal Son of God.

Christians can rejoice that they are redeemed, regenerated, adopted into God's family, forgiven, and made priests and kings. They can realize that they have infinite value in the sight of God, for God allowed His Son to die to pay the penalty for their sins. At the same time, however, we must never forget that "all have sinned and come short of the glory of God," and that "the wages of sin is death." By grace we are saved, and by grace we are allowed to live in relationship to God. God did not give His grace to only one person. Since we are all recipients of grace, it is foolish for any of us to think more highly than he ought. Rather, we should consider others better than ourselves. This follows the example of Christ, and honors a direct command from God.

As we put off pride, we must put on humility and service to others. In recognizing the concerns of others and helping them with those needs we keep our focus on the Lord and others rather than on ourselves. As we subject ourselves "one to another" we heed Peter's injunction to "be clothed with humility" (I Peter 5:5).

Louis Pasteur was praised for finding a vaccine that immunized people against rabies. Everyone is inflicted with a spiritual disease—self-centeredness. But a cure is available. Just as Louis Pasteur was recognized and rewarded for his contributions, so God will reward every believer who purges himself from the sin of self-righteousness and avoids the toxin of pride. Because of our

Romans 3:23; 6:23

Romans 12:3

Remember Mark 10:45: "For even the Son of man came not to be ministered unto, but to minister, and to give his life a ransom for many."

53

Lord's faithfulness, God has "highly exalted him, and given him a name which is above every name" (Philippians 2:9). And God has promised us: "Humble yourselves therefore under the mighty hand of God, that he may exalt you in due time" (I Peter 5:6).

NOW TEST YOUR KNOWLEDGE

Answer true or false:

1. Pride is especially noted by God as a hated sin.
2. A person who has a good opinion of himself is prideful.
3. The cause of pride is self-righteousness.
4. The toxin of pride only affects the individual who is proud.
5. The opposite of pride is self-abasement.
6. God disciplines us when we're prideful because He hates us.
7. Pride is a denial of God's sovereign goodness.
8. Jesus Christ demonstrated good self-esteem and a humble spirit.
9. God will exalt those who maintain a humble spirit.
10. Humility comes by recognizing that our righteousness is from God and from esteeming others better than ourselves.

FOOD FOR THOUGHT

"Of all marvelous things, perhaps there is nothing that angels behold with such supreme astonishment as a proud man."
—Charles Caleb Colton

7

CHANGING THE TRUTH:
THE TOXIN OF LYING
GENESIS 27:1—28:10; PROVERBS 6:17; 12:19,22; 19:5,9;
EPHESIANS 4:14,25

EVERY DAY WITH THE WORD

Monday	Lying's character	Genesis 27:1-19
Tuesday	Lying's cause	Genesis 27:18-27
Wednesday	Lying's condemnation	Proverbs 6:17; 12:19-22; 19:5-9
Thursday	Lying's contradiction	Titus 1
Friday	Lying's consequences	Genesis 27:30—28:10
Saturday	Lying's correction	Colossians 3:9-16
Sunday	Lying's cure	Ephesians 4:15-25

The Bible doesn't spin fairy tales in which all the characters live "happily ever after." Even the most famous Bible characters had weaknesses which are included in the narratives. Until Jacob submitted to God and God transformed him at Penuel, his self-centeredness led him to partake of the deadly toxin of lying.

Think of Adam, Noah, Moses, Joshua, or Saul, and how the reality of their faith, *and sin*, has been preserved in the Scriptures.

DESCRIBING LYING
(Genesis 27:1-29)

By way of review it would be helpful to read Genesis 25—27.

Jacob frequently looked out for number one. The remarkable story of the birth of Jacob and Esau is recorded in Genesis 25. Esau was the first of the twins to be born. He was taken from his mother's womb with Jacob's hand grasping his heel. The name Esau may be derived from a word that means hairy or from a word that means red.

Jacob means "he grasped the heel," and figuratively means supplanter or "he deceives."

Jacob's self-centeredness is depicted clearly in Genesis 26:27-34. The account reveals that Esau was famished from hunting in the open country. When he arrived home he asked Jacob for some of the stew that Jacob was cooking. Esau allowed his hunger to supersede his reason. He willingly offered his birthright in exchange for some of the stew. Of course, Jacob should not have cheated his brother out of his birthright. He should have cared for Esau's needs without charge. But Jacob's self-interest was strong. He gained Esau's birthright by taking advantage of his hunger.

This account is found in Genesis 25:27-34.

A number of years later, in Isaac's old age, Jacob, by the encouragement of his mother Rebekah, acted with guile to deceive his father. We read in Genesis 27:1-4: "And it came to pass, that when Isaac was old, and his eyes were dim, so that he could not see, he called Esau his eldest son, and said unto him, My son: and he said unto him, Behold, here am I. And he said, Behold now, I am old, I know not the day of my death: Now therefore take, I pray thee, thy weapons, thy quiver and thy bow, and go out to the field, and take me some venison: And make me savoury meat, such as I love, and bring it to me, that I may eat; that my soul may bless thee before I die."

With the birthright safely tucked away in her son's pocket, Rebekah encouraged Jacob to deceive Isaac so that he could receive the family blessing. The verses that follow relate how Rebekah made her husband's favorite meal, and then attired Jacob for the deception. Jacob was afraid that his father would recognize him, and he questioned his mother. Jacob was more fearful

The blessing was important, for it would confirm that this son would rule the family in the father's absence and therefore receive a double inheritance.

over the deception than Rebekah was. He was afraid that his father would see through the ruse, and curse him rather than bless him (Genesis 27:12).

In order to make the deception successful, Rebekah clothed Jacob with Esau's raiment. She also put goat skins upon his hands and the smooth part of his neck. She realized that Isaac would have to feel the hairiness and roughness of skin if he were to believe the son was Esau. With disguise in place and food on a tray, Jacob entered Isaac's presence. When Isaac asked who he was, Jacob boldly lied: "I am Esau thy firstborn" (Genesis 27:19). When Isaac questioned how Esau was able to return from the hunt so quickly, Jacob again lied: "Because the Lord thy God brought it to me" (verse 20). Jacob not only displayed insensitivity to his mother and his father but also a lack of any fear of God. Jacob, the deceiver, knew what he wanted, and he did what he had to do to obtain it.

Although Isaac was nearly blind, he still was able to hear.

Still troubled by the situation, Isaac pressed further: "Come near, I pray thee, that I may feel thee, my son, whether thou be my very son Esau or not" (verse 21). Isaac was bothered because the voice of his son was that of Jacob, but after he felt the affixed skins, he was somewhat relieved. However, wanting to be certain of the son's identity, he questioned one more time: "Art thou my very son Esau? And he [Jacob] said, I am" (verse 24). Jacob had lied a third time.

Could it be that Jacob's deceptive character and his desire to supplant his

Trying to settle his doubts, Isaac made one final test. "And his father Isaac said unto him, Come near now, and kiss me, my son. And he came near, and kissed him: and he smelled the smell of his raiment, and blessed him, and said, See, the smell of my son is as the smell of a field which the Lord hath blessed" (verses 26,27). Then Isaac blessed his son Jacob, making him head over his brother, and pronouncing a curse on anyone who cursed him.

brother enhanced Isaac's suspicion?

What is the character of lying? We could say that lying is simply telling "an untruth." However, lying goes further than speaking a falsehood, for it involves all forms of deception. Lying's character, its very nature, is deception.

Why did Jacob lie? Why did he extort his brother's birthright instead of freely alleviating his hunger? Why did he disguise himself and deceive his father? Why did he claim to be Esau, and then blaspheme God in his deception? The answer is his self-centeredness. Jacob wanted to better himself, and that motivation so possessed him that he allowed the toxin of lying to spread within him.

The basis of all sin is selfishness.

Once a lie is told, it has to be confessed or additional lies have to be told to keep the deception going. Such was the case with Jacob. The birthright was important, but he also wanted his father's blessing in order to realize that inheritance. So with lie upon lie, Jacob set out to better his situation. All he needed was a little encouragement from his mother to allow his selfishness to motivate his behavior. Lying's character is deception; its cause is self-betterment.

Can you remember a time when you told a second lie to cover up a deception?

What Rebekah and Jacob failed to realize was that all deceptions are eventually uncovered and lead to tragic results. Rebekah figured that Esau was alone in the field while Isaac was alone in the tent. Because Esau and Isaac were isolated, Jacob would be able to deceive them, she reasoned. But she failed to take God into account. Since God is omnipresent, He was in the field with Esau, in the kitchen with Rebekah, and in Isaac's tent. Nothing was hidden from God. And neither is anything hidden from Him today.

DEFEATING LYING
(Proverbs 6:17; 12:19,22; 19:5,9; Genesis 27:30—28:9; Ephesians 4:15,25)

After Isaac finished blessing his son, Jacob had scarcely left the tent when Esau arrived with a prepared meal. Can you picture the proud son, successful in his hunting and returning to his father, who loved him, to present a tasty meal? This elder son responded immediately to his father's desire and was very likely excited about receiving the official blessing. If there was ever a wet blanket thrown on a situation, if ever an emotion changed from joy to sorrow, it was then.

When Esau approached his father, he said, "Let my father arise, and eat of his son's venison, that thy soul may bless me" (Genesis 27:31). Jacob asked him, "Who are thou?" When Esau identified himself, Isaac began to tremble. He asked: "Who? where is he that taketh venison, and brought it me, and I have eaten of all before thou camest, and have blessed him? yea, and he shall be blessed" (verse 33).

When Esau heard his father's words, he was overwhelmed with emotion. He cried bitter tears. Then Isaac told Esau about Jacob's deception. He said: "Thy brother came with subtilty, and hath taken away thy blessing" (verse 35). Through his tears, Esau responded: "Is not he rightly named Jacob? for he hath supplanted me these two times:

Can you remember a situation where lying produced a strained relationship or lack of trust?

he took away my birthright; and, behold, now he hath taken away my blessing" (verse 36).

God abhors lying (Proverbs 6:17). Hebrews 6:18 states that it is impossible for God to lie. God condemns lying because it is a denial of His very character.

Self-betterment through deception is a deadly toxin. God warns us of the seriousness of lying. "The lip of truth shall be established for ever: but a lying tongue is but for a moment" (Proverbs 12:19). "Lying lips are abomination to the Lord: but they that deal truly are his delight" (verse 22). "A false witness shall not be unpunished, and he that speaketh lies shall not escape" (Proverbs 19:5).

God hates lying because it denies His character, but as we can see from what transpired in Isaac's family, it also destroys love and fellowship. How did Esau feel about being deceived? How do you feel when you are deceived? He was hurt, bitter, angry, and vengeful. Genesis 27:41 relates: "And Esau hated Jacob because of the blessing wherewith his father blessed him: and Esau said in his heart, The days of mourning for my father are at hand; then will I slay my brother Jacob." When Rebekah heard Esau's words, she told Jacob to flee and protect himself "until thy brother's fury turn away; Until thy brother's anger turn away from thee, and he forget that which thou hast done to him" (verses 44,45).

The consequences of lying are separation and hatred. Because of Jacob's deception, hatred was kindled between Esau and Jacob and between Esau and his parents. The deception also caused a physical separation between Jacob and his family.

"A false witness shall not be unpunished, and he that speaketh lies shall perish." God will judge lying, in fact, no liar will be a citizen of the New Jerusalem (Revelation 21:27; 22:15).

Satan is called the deceiver; God is truth. Satan would have brother slander brother but God would have us speak the truth in love.

Rebekah could not have known that the toxin of lying would prohibit her from ever seeing her favorite son again. Jacob never imagined how the poison of lying could have produced a hatred within his brother.

Knowing that lying destroys lives, God commands His children to communicate honestly with one another. He wants us to put off falsehood and to speak the truth. Whether a person is tempted to deceive by lying occasionally or by lying so often that it becomes a deeply ingrained habit, the principles of resistance and replacement also apply to this toxin, lying. As we put off lying, we must put on the truth. Ephesians 4:14,15 admonishes: "That we henceforth be no more children, tossed to and fro, and carried about by every wind of doctrine, by the sleight of men, and cunning craftiness, whereby they lie in wait to deceive; But speaking the truth in love, may grow up into him in all things, which is the head, even Christ." Rather than saying anything that is not truthful, we can speak the truth in love.

Building on the fact that Christians are one in the Body of Christ, Paul admonishes: "Wherefore putting away lying, speak every man truth with his neighbour: for we are members one of another" (Ephesians 4:25). What will keep us from imbibing the toxin of lying? First, a good understanding of the nature of God will protect us. Second, a sincere desire to honor the God of truth will protect us. Then, third, we need a healthy appreciation of the interdependence among the members of the body of Christ and the importance of honesty in our relationships with people. Lying causes separation and hatred, but

"But speaking the truth in love, may grow up into him in all things, which is the head, even Christ" (Ephesians 4:15).

speaking the truth produces unity and trust.

The Bible introduces us to individuals who tried to better themselves through deception. To name just a few, Satan, Abraham, Jacob, David, Peter, and Ananias and Sapphira lied to better themselves. But they all learned the destructive results of lying. Lying for the purpose of self-betterment is an illusion. Believers who truly want to receive the best that God has for them will avoid the deception of the adversary.

See III John 4.

NOW TEST YOUR KNOWLEDGE

Fill in the blanks:

1. "These six things doth the Lord hate: yea, seven are an abomination to him; a proud look, a _____ _____ . . . ."
2. "And Esau _____ Jacob because of the blessing wherewith his father blessed him . . . ."
3. "Wherefore putting away _____ speak every man _____ with his neighbour: for we are members one of another."
4. "A false witness shall not be unpunished, and he that speaketh lies _____ _____ _____ ."
5. "Be sure your _____ will find you out."

Match the following:

6. Lying's character
7. Lying's cause
8. Lying's condemnation
9. Lying's consequences
10. Lying's cure

A. Separation and hatred
B. Speaking the truth
C. Deception
D. Self-betterment
E. God is truth

FOOD FOR THOUGHT

"A lie is like a snowball; the longer it is rolled, the larger it is."

—Martin Luther

NEVER ENOUGH:
THE TOXIN OF GREED
JOSHUA 7; PROVERBS 15:27; 28:16; MATTHEW 6:19-34;
26:14-16; 27:3-5; MARK 7:20-23; ACTS 5:1-11;
COLOSSIANS 3:1-6

Learn by Heart:
"For where your treasure is, there will your heart be also" (Matthew 6:21).

EVERY DAY WITH THE WORD

Monday	Achan and greed	Joshua 7
Tuesday	Judas and greed	Matthew 26:47-56
Wednesday	Ananias and greed	Acts 5:1-11
Thursday	The company greed keeps	Mark 7:20-23
Friday	The essence of greed	Colossians 3:1-6
Saturday	The result of greed	I Timothy 6:1-10
Sunday	Deliverance from greed	Matthew 6:19-34

One of the words a child learns earliest is "more." Some children grow into the teen years, then into adulthood, with the same fixation for more. While the desire for more is not wrong in itself, when it is a consuming passion for things, clearly the toxin of greed is present. The adversary has been very successful in destroying people's lives with greed. In both the Old and New Testaments we can find—

How would you answer the question: "When is enough enough?"

EXAMPLES OF GREED
(Joshua 7; Matthew 26:14-16; 27:3-5;
Acts 5:1-11)

As the Israelites crossed the Jordan River, they brought with them both the presence of God and the law of God. In the Ten Commandments God had warned them not to covet anything belonging to someone else. As the Israelites approached Jericho, God warned them that all the wealth of Jericho was to be devoted to Him. Their giving of the spoils of this first battle into the Lord's treasury was a symbol (like the tithe) that God was their Provider.

Exodus 20:17

Joshua 6 records the fall of Jericho. However, chapter 7 begins with this sad comment: "But the children of Israel committed a trespass in the accursed thing: for Achan, the son of Carmi, the son of Zabdi, the son of Zerah, of the tribe of Judah, took of the accursed thing: and the anger of the Lord was kindled against the children of Israel" (verse 1).

See Joshua 6:17-19.

Caught up in the thrill of victory over the fall of Jericho, Joshua thought it necessary to use only part of the army to attack lesser fortified Ai. When the Israelites fled in defeat, Joshua inquired of the Lord, and the Lord responded: "Israel hath sinned, and they have also transgressed my covenant which I have commanded them: for they have even taken of the accursed thing, and have also stolen, and dissembled also, and they have put it even among their own stuff" (verse 11). Some greedy person in the camp had stolen what belonged to the Lord. His greed had contributed to Israel's defeat.

It is interesting to note that Israel went into battle against Ai without waiting on the Lord. What presumption!

Joshua warned the people that the person who was caught with the "accursed thing" would be destroyed. Achan had a chance to confess his sin, but he didn't until the next morning—after the lot revealed that he was the offender. Verses 20,21 indicate "And Achan answered Joshua, and said, Indeed I have sinned against the Lord God of Israel, and thus and thus have I done: When I saw among the spoils a goodly Babylonish garment,

Just as all Israel stood guilty before God because of Achan's sin, so Achan's entire family was guilty because of his act. The text does not indicate the age of the family members; likely

they all were
aware of the
buried treasure.

and two hundred shekels of silver, and a wedge of gold fifty shekels weight, then I coveted them, and took them; and, behold, they are hid in the earth in the midst of my tent, and the silver under it." Achan knew that the spoils he had hidden beneath his tent belonged to God, yet he kept silent until he was discovered. As judgment upon Achan, and as an example to the Israelites, Achan and his family were stoned in the valley of Achor.

The betrayal
price was "thirty
pieces of silver"
(Matthew 26:15;
27:3).

In the Gospels we see greed as the reason Judas was willing to betray the Lord. Judas asked the chief priests: "What will ye give me, and I will deliver him unto you?" (Matthew 20:15). Judas' desire for personal profit—his "love of money"—was stronger than his love for Christ.

Another illustration of the toxin of greed can be seen in an event that happened in the early church. Because of the joy of their salvation and their first commitment to Christ, the Jerusalem believers were willing to share their material well-being with others. Following the example of Barnabas, Ananias and Sapphira also sold some property and made a gift to the ministry. The motivation of their heart was wrong, however. They pretended that gift was the entire amount received from the sale of their property. Their act resulted in judgment. The Holy Spirit made Peter aware that Ananias had deceived the church. Peter said, "Ananias, why hath Satan filled thine heart to lie to the Holy Ghost, and to keep back part of the price of the land?" (Acts 5:3). The adversary had successfully assaulted Ananias with the toxins of lying and greed.

See Acts 4:36,37:
"And Joses, who
by the apostles
was surnamed
Barnabas...
Having land, sold
it, and brought
the money, and
laid it at the
apostles feet."

Peter pointed out that while the land remained his, it was at his own disposal. In fact, after he sold the land, he still had freedom to use the money in whatever manner he wished. But Ananias wanted his money and also coveted the praise and recognition of the church. His greed kept him from presenting a pure gift, as Barnabas had done earlier.

Gifts are to be offered cheerfully, not under compulsion (II Corinthians 9:7).

After hearing Peter's words of judgment, Ananias died and was buried. Shortly after, his wife Sapphira told the same lie to the church. "Then Peter said unto her, How is it that ye have agreed together to tempt the Spirit of the Lord? behold, the feet of them which have buried thy husband are at the door, and shall carry thee out. Then fell she down straightway at his feet, and yielded up the ghost: and the young men came in, and found her dead, and, carrying her forth, buried her by her husband" (verses 9,10).

Ananias and Sapphira were possessed by greed. This sin led to the toxin of lying. In addition, they were overcome by pride and the desire for recognition. While Ananias and Sapphira may have sincerely wanted to give a gift, they also wanted to do the "in thing." Their greed kept them from offering a sincere, full gift.

THE ESSENCE OF GREED
(Proverbs 15:27; 28:16; Mark 7:20-23)

Greed comes out of a person's heart. Jesus said, "For from within, out of the heart of men, proceed evil thoughts, adulteries, fornications, murders, thefts, covetousness, wickedness, deceit, lasciviousness, an evil eye, blasphemy, pride, foolishness: All these evil things come from within and defile the man" (Mark 7:21-23). To the church at Colosse Paul presented a similar list of sins,

Notice also
Ephesians 5:3-5.

including greed (covetousness). Paul labeled these behaviors as "idolatry" (Colossians 3:5,6). The person who covets—the greedy individual—is an idolater. His idols are the possessions he so eagerly craves.

The adversary's desire is to defile believers, and he uses the lusts of the sin nature to harm us. The toxin of greed can enter our system and turn a legitimate concern into an out-of-control lust. Who can question the value of an IRA, a nice home, a dependable automobile, or the need for fashionable clothing? But if a person is never content with the amount of money in an IRA, if his home is never large enough, if he wants a newer car because his is a couple of years old, or if he must have the best in designer fashions, then he needs to question whether greed's poison is at work.

When we think of a greedy person, we think of the wealthy miser, but covetous people abound at all socio-economic levels. A teenager might have a burning passion for his own automobile; a poor man, his own colored television; and a wealthy man, financial security at age 40. Having financial goals is not a sin. But, placing these goals above godly contentment, or before honoring God with our treasures, is sin. The rich young ruler's sin was not that he was rich, but that he put his wealth ahead of following Christ.

Material planning
is appropriate,
but contentment
must have a
deeper basis.
Paul testified:
"Not that I speak
in respect of
want: for I have
learned, in
whatsoever state
I am, therewith to
be content. I
know both how to
be abased, and I
know how to
abound: every

Because greed is idolatry, the Bible repeatedly warns against the love of money. First Timothy 6:10 states: "For the love of money is the root of all evil: which while some coveted after, they have erred from the faith, and pierced themselves through with many sorrows." This verse has often been misquoted to say that "money is the root of all evil." The text says that it is "the love of money" that is the root of all evil. There is nothing wrong with money. In fact, the Scriptures admonish us to work so that we are able to care for financial needs. But when the earning of money or the acquiring of possessions becomes an obsession, likely the toxin of greed has poisoned both our thinking and affections.

The result of greed is clear. Paul told Timothy that the love of money, which some coveted after, had led them to err from the faith and be pierced through with many sorrows. Further, greed hurts more than the transgressor. "He that is greedy of gain troubleth his own house" (Proverbs 15:27). Both family and friends of the greedy pay dearly for this self-centered aim.

Greed is like the illusive carrot that dangles in front of a donkey. The animal moves continually with the thought that satisfaction is just one step ahead. For the covetous person, however, there is never satisfaction ahead, for there is always that desire for just one more carrot. At the end of 70 years of stockpiling things, the greedy Christian may finally realize how much he lost by not building a deep relationship with his God and with his brothers and sisters.

ELIMINATING GREED
(Matthew 6:19-34; Colossians 3:1-3)

Although the Pharisees had hundreds of regulations on how to please God, Jesus summarized man's responsibility by stating: "Thou shalt love the Lord thy God with all thy heart, and with all thy soul, and with all thy strength, and with all thy mind; and thy neighbour as thyself"

where and in all things I am instructed both to be full and to be hungry, both to abound and to suffer need. I can do all things through Christ which strengtheneth me" (Philippians 4:11-13).

By contrast there is well-being for the faithful, for "he that hateth covetousness shall prolong his days" (Proverbs 28:16b).

Whenever something becomes a god, it leads us away from sincere faith. In turn, when we do not walk a life of faith, we lose our purpose and power, our peace and joy.

Our daily focus must be on God, rather than on things. Study Luke 10:27.

(Luke 10:27). Jesus did not state that it was all right to own one donkey but wrong to own two. He didn't state that owning a one-room home was commendable but owning a large home (like that of Mary, the mother of John Mark) was wrong. The key issue was to love God with everything within us and to love our neighbors as ourselves. There is nothing wrong with having five coats, but if our neighbor needs one, we should give him one of them.

See Matthew 5:40.

We can gain victory over greed by having a balanced source of information about the material world and by maintaining a deep devotion to God. To the church at Colosse Paul wrote: "If ye then be risen with Christ, seek those things which are above, where Christ sitteth on the right hand of God. Set your affections on things above, not on things on the earth. For ye are dead, and your life is hid with Christ in God" (Colossians 3:1-3). We Christians are citizens of Heaven. We are living temporarily on earth. While we might repaint, paper, and make other improvements to a wrecked home, we are reluctant to make major costly repairs to a temporary residence. In the same way, we have to comprehend that we are a terminal people. Even the young child is living a life that is terminal. So we need to set our affections above where Christ is seated. We see the futility of pursuing materialism when we read Ecclesiastes. The Scriptures display the tragic results of greed in the lives of Achan, Judas, Ananias and Sapphira, and others.

"For what is your life? It is even a vapour, that appeareth for a little time, and then vanisheth away" (James 4:14).

Jesus taught: "Lay not up for yourselves treasures upon earth, where moth and rust doth corrupt, and where thieves break through and steal: But lay up for yourselves treasures in heaven, where neither moth nor rust doth corrupt, and where thieves do not break through nor steal; For where your treasure is, there will your heart be also" (Matthew 6:19-21). There is nothing wrong with providing financially for our children or our future. Actually, the Scriptures commend this type of faithful stewardship. But we need a continual concentration of our resources on heavenly things in order to keep greed in check.

You cannot have both God and money. See Matthew 6:24.

The command of Christ is clear: "But seek ye first the kingdom of God, and his righteousness; and all these things shall be added unto you" (Matthew 6:33).

NOW TEST YOUR KNOWLEDGE

Answer true or false:

1. God wants all Christians to be wealthy.
2. Paul learned to be content when he had much and when he had little.
3. The toxin of greed is related to the lust of the eye.
4. We cannot love both God and money.
5. Ananias and Sapphira had to give all their money to God.
6. God will provide for all our needs as we trust Him to do so.
7. Things that we covet are idols.
8. Greed should be confessed as sin.
9. Studying the Scriptures and studying the needy world around will lead us away from greed.
10. Devotion to Christ will keep our hearts right.

FOOD FOR THOUGHT

"He is no fool who gives what he cannot keep, to gain what he cannot lose!"
—Jim Elliott

THE SILENT TREATMENT:
THE TOXIN OF PRAYERLESSNESS
PROVERBS 3:5,6; MATTHEW 6:5-8; MARK 11:22-26; 14:38;
LUKE 18:9-14; 22:40-46; ACTS 4:31; ROMANS 10:13;
PHILIPPIANS 4:6,7; I THESSALONIANS 5:17,18; I JOHN 1:8,9

Learn by Heart:
"Praying always
with all prayer
and supplication
in the Spirit, and
watching
thereunto with all
perseverance
and supplication
for all saints"
(Ephesians 6:18).

EVERY DAY WITH THE WORD

Monday	Urgency in prayer	Luke 18:1-8
Tuesday	Importance of prayer	Romans 10:13; I John 1:9; Mark 14:38; Acts 4:31; Proverbs 3:5,6
Wednesday	Example of prayer	Mark 1:35; Luke 5:15,16; Matthew 26:39,42,44
Thursday	Power of prayer	Matthew 17:14-21
Friday	Hindrances to prayer	Psalm 66:18; Isaiah 59:1,2; Matthew 5:23,24; James 4:2-4
Saturday	Attitudes and prayer	I Thessalonians 5:16-28
Sunday	Actions and prayer	Philippians 4:4-8; Matthew 6:5-13

Have you taken
time to evaluate
your prayer life,
as was suggested
at the end of last
week's class
session?

"Prayer really isn't that important." That statement would be labeled heretical if it were made from the pulpit or suggested in a Bible class. Unfortunately, the statement seems to be confirmed by the daily practice of many Christians. How important is prayer? Won't God pursue His purposes whether I pray or not? In what way is prayer necessary for my life? These questions are answered as we study—

THE PRIORITY OF PRAYER
(Luke 22:40,46; Romans 10:13; I John 1:8,9; Acts 4:31; Mark 11:22-26; 14:38; Proverbs 3:5,6)

Throughout our study we have been observing that believers are in a warfare against a subtle enemy. Satan would like to poison us by appealing to us through the lust of the flesh, the lust of the eye, and the pride of life. He tries to gain victory not only through offensive assaults, but also by weakening our defenses. If he can break down our resistance, he will soon defeat us; we will fall into sin.

Recognizing Satan's subtlety Jesus warned His disciples: "Pray that ye enter not into temptation" (Luke 22:40). Twice on that evening in Gethsemane, Jesus told His disciples to be vigilant in prayer, lest they be overcome by the adversary. Both our Lord's instructions and example prove the cruciality of prayer.

Jesus recognized that prayerful vigilance was difficult, but His command remains: "Watch ye and pray, lest ye enter into temptation. The Spirit truly is ready, but the flesh is weak" (Mark 14:38).

Prayer is communication with God. Good communication is essential in husband-wife relationships, parent-child relationships, and employer-employee relationships. Daily, people make statements to one another, ask questions, make requests, speak words of appreciation, and apologize when an apology is needed. So too, in our relationship with our heavenly Father, we communicate through all types of prayer: adoration, thanksgiving, confession, and supplication.

In intercessory prayer we make petition for others.

A person cannot become a Christian unless he *asks* Jesus Christ to be his Saviour and Lord (Romans 10:9-13). Nor can a believer walk in unbroken fellowship, unless he acknowledges his disobedience (I John 1:9). The Christian life is lived by prayer. The Bible tells us how to live; prayer empowers us to live.

Jesus told His followers that prayer is essential for victory over the adversary (see Mark 14:38). By His own example He demonstrated the priority of prayer. At the beginning of His ministry He prayed (Mark 1:35). Before selecting His disciples He prayed (Luke 6:12). Before He performed miracles He prayed (John 11:41,42). Before He ate He prayed (John 6:11). Before He left His disciples He prayed (John 17). In preparing His heart in the garden of Gethsemane He prayed (Mark 14:35-42). And, while He hung on the cross, He prayed (Luke 23:34). Jesus' whole life serves as an example of prayer.

Moved by Jesus' example, the disciples asked: "Lord, teach us to pray, as John also taught his disciples" (Luke 11:1). In response, Jesus taught them what is called "the Lord's Prayer," better called "the Disciples' Prayer," because Jesus offered it as an example for them. The fact that they asked Jesus to instruct them on this subject shows that they recognized prayer as a priority in His life.

The adversary's strategy is to isolate and assault believers. He desires to cut our line of communication with Headquarters. He does not want God to receive our affection. He wants us to be bound with guilt, or to maintain an unforgiving spirit. He rejoices when a child of God walks naively into temptation rather than being delivered from evil.

Jesus taught a remarkable lesson on prayer one morning when He and His disciples passed a withered fig tree. Mark 11:22-26 records: "And Jesus answering saith unto them, Have faith in

The Lord's Prayer is recorded in Matthew 6:9-13 and Luke 11:2-4. The content of the prayer shows the importance of reverence for God, appreciation for His goodness, and a commitment on the part of the believer to align himself with God's will.

73

God. For verily I say unto you, That whosoever shall say unto this mountain, Be thou removed, and be thou cast into the sea; and shall not doubt in his heart, but shall believe that those things which he saith shall come to pass; he shall have whatsoever he saith. Therefore I say unto you, What things soever ye desire, when ye pray, believe that ye receive them, and ye shall have them. And when ye stand praying, forgive, if ye have ought against any: that your Father also which is in heaven may forgive you your trespasses. But if ye do not forgive, neither will your Father which is in heaven forgive your trespasses." In cursing the fig tree, the Teacher of prayer was again giving instructions to the students of prayer. Those who "have faith in God" (verse 24) and are in right relationship with God and others (verses 25,26) can ask God for great things. The promise of answered prayer extends to "whosoever."

Does God want us to resist the adversary? Does He want us to be victorious over temptation? Does He want us to know His love and goodness? The obvious answer is yes, and prayer is the essential means for obtaining this victory and blessing. Most Christians, however, do not believe that by prayer they could literally remove a mountain. If prayer could be exercised with that degree of success, then Christians would not tolerate ungodly rulers. They would never have material needs. They would never lose their sporting contests. And rain would never fall on their picnics or parades. We can receive what we ask for in faith, but our belief must be tempered by the will of God. The problem for most of us is not that we ask for too much but for too little, or

The cursed fig tree was an illustration of Israel, who was to be fruitful, but in reality was barren.

Jesus was a master of illustrations. He used natural occurrences in life to show timeless principles.

The Bible gives several reasons why prayers are hindered. Psalm 66:18; Isaiah 59:1,2; Matthew 5:23,24; Matthew 6:9,15.

we ask with the wrong motives (see James 4:2-4). Just as Jesus did not want James and John to call down fire from heaven upon Samaria, neither does He want all the mountains in the world leveled. Effective prayer is based upon a sincere desire that God's will be done. We must yield to God's superior wisdom when we pray. He knows what is best. Proverbs 3:5,6 says: "Trust in the Lord with all thine heart; and lean not unto thine own understanding. In all thy ways acknowledge him, and he shall direct thy paths."

THE PRACTICE OF PRAYER
(Matthew 6:5-8; Luke 18:9-14; Philippians 4:6,7; I Thessalonians 5:17,18)

Men and women who desire a deep relationship with God and a life of effectiveness for God must maintain regular communication with Him. If we are to be people of prayer, we need to develop right attitudes in prayer and practical habits of prayer.

Pray believing. When Jesus entered Capernaum, a centurion asked Jesus to heal his sick servant. When Jesus offered to go and heal him, the centurion replied: "Lord, I am not worthy that thou shouldest come under my roof: but speak the word only, and my servant shall be healed" (Matthew 8:8). The soldier recognized the principle of authority and submission, and realized that Jesus had authority over sickness. "When Jesus heard it, he marvelled, and said to them that followed, Verily I say unto you, I have not found so great faith, no, not in Israel . . . . And Jesus said unto the centurion, Go thy way; and as thou hast believed, so be it done unto thee. And his servant

"But let him ask in faith, nothing wavering. For he that wavereth is like a wave of the sea driven with the wind and tossed. For let not that man think that he shall receive any thing of the Lord" (James 1:6,7).

was healed in the selfsame hour" (verses 10,13). The centurion demonstrated that wholehearted belief that Christ could accomplish what he asked. We, too, must believe that God can grant our petitions.

Pray thankfully. "In every thing give thanks: for this is the will of God in Christ Jesus concerning you" (I Thessalonians 5:18). The adversary's toxins of envy, greed, and complaining lose all impact on the believer who prays with a thankful heart. Thanksgiving is more than just the expressing of appreciation to God for what He has provided. It is also the bringing of requests to Him with an attitude of appreciation for whatever answer He may give. While we may ask for a specific outcome, more than anything we desire His perfect will. Therefore, we are able to come to Him in prayer with thanksgiving, fully confident of His goodness on our behalf.

Pray humbly. In the parable of the Pharisee and the publican (Luke 18:10-14), Jesus emphasized the difference between the self-righteous Pharisee and the humble publican. The attitude of the publican was commended by the Saviour. The publican prayed: "Be merciful to me a sinner." This resulted in his obtaining mercy. The Pharisee displayed a proud attitude. He received nothing from God.

A prevalent teaching insists that Christians should demand things from God. The rationale is that, since we are God's children and invited to come boldly before the throne of grace, we can demand our inheritance and rights. While it is true that God has given us many promises and blessings, a demanding, self-centered attitude is not taught in the Scriptures. Rather, God exalts

Hebrews 4:16 teaches that we can come boldly to God in prayer, but we must also come with humility ("to obtain mercy, and find grace to help in time of need").

the humble, who recognize His greatness and goodness.

In the Old Testament God promised: "If my people, which are called by my name, shall humble themselves, and pray, and seek my face, and turn from their wicked ways; then will I hear from heaven, and will forgive their sin, and will heal their land" (II Chronicles 7:14). While that promise was made specifically to Israel, the principle of coming to God in humble prayer remains for all generations. In the words of James, "God resisteth the proud, and giveth grace to the humble" (James 4:6b). Effective prayer displays an attitude of humility.

Pray honestly. Have you noticed how Jesus welcomed sinners yet often spoke harshly to the religious Pharisees? In Matthew 6:5-8 He instructed: "When thou prayest, thou shalt not be as the hypocrites are: for they love to pray standing in the synagogues and in the corners of the streets, that they may be seen of men. Verily I say unto you, They have their reward. But thou, when thou prayest, enter into thy closet, and when thou hast shut thy door, pray to thy Father which is in secret; and thy Father which seeth in secret shall reward thee openly. But when ye pray, use not vain repetitions, as the heathen do: for they think that they shall be heard for their much speaking. Be not ye therefore like unto them: for your Father knoweth what things ye have need of, before ye ask him."

The Pharisees loved to spin off long prayers so that people would be impressed with their knowledge and spirituality. Their prayers were not their communication to God, but were a hypocritical display before the people. Jesus admonished that our prayers are to come from an honest heart desiring to communicate with Him.

Pray specifically. Paul told believers to pray specifically. He instructed: "Be careful for nothing; but in every thing by prayer and supplication with thanksgiving let your requests be made known unto God" (Philippians 4:6). The very thing that would make us anxious should be the basis for making our request known unto God. When we are anxious, we need His peace. Happily, when we pray honestly and specifically, God gives us His peace.

Pray continually. Daniel prayed at least three times a day (Daniel 6:10). The psalmist prayed every morning and noon (Psalm 55:17). If we are to be successful over the adversary, we must have a consciousness of God which pervades our day. This is the meaning of "Pray without ceasing" (I Thessalonians 5:17). Each day is to be lived with the realization of God's presence through ongoing communication with Him through regular periods of prayer or impromptu offerings of praise and petition.

A prayerless Christian is a deceived and weak Christian. The adversary can slowly poison him because his defenses have been weakened. But the believer who follows the teaching and example of Christ will pray believing, thankfully, humbly, honestly, specifically, and continually. Martin Luther said, "Prayer is a strong wall and fortress of the church; it is a goodly Christian weapon." If we use the weapon of prayer in our fight with the adversary, we will be victorious.

"Casting all your care upon him; for he careth for you" (I Peter 5:7).

Prayerful recitation of the Scriptures is a form of meditation. Notice in Psalm 119 how frequently David practiced this type of prayer.

NOW TEST YOUR KNOWLEDGE

Complete the following:

1. "Pray without _____."
2. "_____ ye and _____, lest ye enter into temptation."
3. "...one of his disciples said unto him, Lord, _____ us to _____, as John taught his disciples."
4. Therefore I say unto you, What things soever ye desire, when ye pray, _____ that ye receive them, and ye shall have them."
5. "Be careful for nothing; but in every thing by _____ and _____ with _____ let your _____ be made known unto God."

Match the following:

6. Supplication _____
7. Intercession _____
8. Confession _____
9. Adoration _____
10. Thanksgiving _____

A. Expressing appreciation to God for His goodness and blessings
B. Praying for the needs of another
C. Bring petitions or requests before God
D. Agreeing with God regarding sin
E. Praising God for who He is

FOOD FOR THOUGHT

"If I should neglect prayer but a single day, I should lose a great deal of the fire of faith."
—Martin Luther

10

THINKING LIKE A NATURAL MAN:
THE TOXIN OF WRONG THINKING
NUMBERS 13; 14; JOSHUA 14:6-14; I SAMUEL 17:1-58;
PROVERBS 2:6; 3:13-18; ROMANS 8:5-9; II CORINTHIANS
10:3-5; EPHESIANS 4:17-19; PHILIPPIANS 4:8,9

EVERY DAY WITH THE WORD

Monday	The mind matters	Romans 12:1-3
Tuesday	The natural mind	I Corinthians 2:9-14
Wednesday	The renewed mind	Romans 8:5-9
Thursday	Controlling thoughts	I Peter 1:13-16
Friday	Maintaining healthy attitudes	I Samuel 17
Saturday	Maintaining realistic attitudes	Joshua 14:6-14
Sunday	Pursuing wisdom	Proverbs 3:13-18

Learn by Heart:
"Finally, brethren, whatsoever things are true, whatsoever things are honest, whatsoever things are just, whatsoever things are pure, whatsoever things are lovely, whatsoever things are of good report: if there be any virtue, and if there be any praise, think on these things" (Philippians 4:8).

See Matthew 15:19.

The old adage is true: "Sow a thought, reap an attitude; sow an attitude, reap an act; sow an act, reap a habit; sow a habit, reap a character; sow a character, reap a destiny." The Bible teaches that the mind is very important. The way we think determines the way we behave. The writer of Proverbs 23:7 wrote: "As he thinketh in his heart, so is he."

YOUR MIND DOES MATTER
(Ephesians 4:17-19; Romans 8:5-9)

Since actions are based on our thoughts and feelings, it's crucial to be able to distinguish right thinking from faulty thinking. Commenting on this, W. Edgar Moore says: "The damage a mind-set can do is dramatically illustrated by the sinking of the *Titanic* on her maiden voyage in

This illustration is from Moore's book, *Creative and Critical Thinking*, and is quoted in *The Christian Use of Emotional Power* by Norman Wright.

Read the descent of man in Romans 1:18-32.

I Corinthians 2:14

I Corinthians 2:15,16

"Behold, I was shapen in iniquity; and in sin did my mother conceive me" (Psalm 51:5).

1912, with the loss of 1,513 lives. Designed to be the safest ship afloat, the *Titanic* was equipped with a double bottom and sixteen watertight compartments. A mind-set that she was unsinkable seems to have been largely responsible for the disaster."

Everyone has a mind set. However, believers do not walk any longer "in the vanity of their mind, Having the understanding darkened, being alienated from the life of God through the ignorance that is in them, because of the blindness of their heart" (Ephesians 4:17,18). Non-believers are carnally minded, but Christians can be spiritually minded. "But ye are not in the flesh, but in the Spirit, if so be that the Spirit of God dwell in you. Now if any man have not the Spirit of Christ, he is none of His" (Romans 8:9). The natural man's mind is short-circuited by sin.

Christians are indeed different! They are no longer to think like natural men, for their minds have been enlightened by the Spirit of God. Paul explained this difference when he wrote: "For they that are after the flesh do mind the things of the flesh; but they that are after the Spirit the thing of the Spirit" (Romans 8:5).

Because all people are born with a sin nature, they inherit a mind that is marred in understanding. But when a person is born anew, the Spirit of God begins to renew his mind. So every child of God is capable of right thinking.

There is much written today about positive thinking. Some writers would have us believe we can do anything we put our minds to. While it is true that most people are plagued by negative thinking and are limited in their accomplishments, the promises of the positive thinkers may also err to an extreme. The Christian who commits his mind to the Lord will be able to maintain a balance that demonstrates "reality thinking."

Reality thinking is not an optimistic, pie-in-the-sky, wishful positivism. Neither is it a self-defeating negativism. It is the rejection of thinking like a natural man and the acceptance of thinking which follows Biblical teaching about reality and our possibilities.

Satan used rationalization in his temptation of Eve. Today he continues to attack the thinking process. If we are to gain victory over the toxin of natural thinking, we must remember the importance of renewing our minds. Paul wrote: "And be not conformed to this world: but be ye transformed by the renewing of your mind, that ye may prove what is that good, and acceptable, and perfect, will of God" (Romans 12:2).

> Reality thinking is based on data from both the natural and supernatural realms. Humanistic psychology and science are limited in that they only study the finite.

YOUR MIND CAN MATURE
(II Corinthians 10:3-5; Philippians 4:8,9; Numbers 13,14; Joshua 14:6-14; I Samuel 17:1-58; Proverbs 2:6; 3:13-18)

The joy of birth and the blessing of a new child would turn to sorrow if the child never grew beyond infancy. The natural biological process generates people into adulthood, and similarly the spiritual process should promote new babes into Christlike maturity. Spiritual growth will take place in our Christian lives as we control our thoughts, maintain healthy attitudes, and pursue wisdom.

Whereas the natural man is incapable of right thinking, the child of God is expected to develop a

> "Wherefore gird up the loins of your mind, be sober, and hope to the end for the grace that is to be brought unto you at the revelation of Jesus Christ" (I Peter 1:13).

See Ephesians 4:22-24.

disciplined control of his thoughts. The principle of replacement is critical for the development of positive thinking. On the negative side we are to bring down imaginations and thoughts that are dishonoring to God (II Corinthians 10:5). On the positive side, we are to replace them with healthy thoughts. Paul admonished: "Finally, brethren, whatsoever things are true, whatsoever things are honest, whatsoever things are pure, whatsoever things are lovely, whatsoever things are of good report; if there be any virtue, and if there be any praise, think on these things" (Philippians 4:8).

Our thoughts are like building blocks; they are "single units of mental action." As we build our thoughts, they develop into attitudes, which are combinations of thoughts. We all have attitudes. We have attitudes regarding the use of time, our work, our rights, our family, and our relationship with God. Negative attitudes are paralyzing; positive attitudes are liberating. Two events in Old Testament history illustrate this principle.

In Numbers 13 and 14 we read the account of the twelve spies who investigated the land of Canaan. Ten of the spies focused on the problems before them, and reported, "We be not able to go up against the people; for they are stronger than we" (Numbers 13:31b). However, two men gave a positive report which affirmed God's omnipotence. Joshua admonished: "If the Lord delight in us, then he will bring us into this land, and give it us; a land which floweth with milk and honey" (Numbers 14:8). Joshua and Caleb demonstrated a belief in God which preserved them while all other adults died in the wilderness.

In I Samuel 17 we read the account of a battle between the Israelites and their perennial enemy,

When Israel finally entered the land, Caleb asked for the hill country, believing God could provide it for him. He said: " ... if so be the LORD will be with me, then I shall be able to drive them out, as the LORD said" (Joshua 14:12b).

the Philistines. The battle lines had been drawn and the armies were at a standoff. Every day a giant warrior, Goliath, came out and challenged God's people. Enveloped in negative thinking, King Saul sat quaking in his tent. We read: "When Saul and all Israel heard those words of the Philistine, they were dismayed, and greatly afraid" (I Samuel 17:11). Saul had tried to encourage someone to fight the giant by promising him great wealth and his daughter in marriage. Nevertheless, every time the Philistine of Gath came out to challenge them, they fled in fear before him (verses 24,25).

Meanwhile, a young boy, David, was sent by his father to bring food to his brothers who were in Israel's army. When David became aware of Israel's situation, he questioned: "Who is this uncircumcised Philistine, that he should defy the armies of the living God?" (verse 26). When Saul had heard that there was a man willing to fight against Goliath, he encouraged David to use his military equipment. However, David had the attitude that God was his Protector and the one who gave victory in battle.

David had experienced the Lord's deliverance earlier in his life when he had killed a lion and a bear who had attacked his father's sheep.

The outcome of the battle of David and Goliath is history, but we sometimes overlook the attitude that made David's victory possible. "This day will the Lord deliver thee into mine hand; and I will smite thee, and take thine head from thee; and I will give the carcasses of the host of the Philistines this day unto the fowls of the air, and to the wild beasts of the earth; that all the earth may know that there is a God in Israel" (verse 46). Saul's thoughts were focused on the size of the giant, and on his own limitations. David's thoughts were focused on the size of his God and on God's ability through him. Saul's attitude was one of fear and defeat; David's attitude was positive and anticipated victory. David knew the reality of the truth spoken centuries later by Paul: "I can do all things through Christ which strengtheneth me" (Philippians 4:13).

Our minds will mature in Christlikeness as we focus on a third concern, and this is growth in wisdom. The book of Proverbs is replete with teaching on the importance of wisdom. For example we read, "Happy is the man that findeth wisdom, and the man that getteth understanding. For the merchandise of it is better than the merchandise of silver, and the gain thereof than fine gold. She is more precious than rubies: and all the things thou canst desire are not to be compared unto her. Length of days is in her right hand; and in her left hand riches and honour" (Proverbs 3:13-16). The value of wisdom is beyond silver, gold or other precious stones. God is the one who provides wisdom (Proverbs 2:6), and He gives it so that His children will enjoy a rich life (Proverbs 16:22).

Just as Saul sat in his tent fearful of his adversary, so the devil would like believers to sit helpless because they think their situations are too difficult. Thinking like a natural man will poison a Christian. The toxin of wrong thinking will sap the Christian's vitality.

As we think, we become. Therefore it is imperative that we think about ourselves as God thinks. The adversary's toxin of wrong thinking can be rendered harmless by controlling our thoughts, maintaining healthy attitudes, and pursuing understanding and wisdom.

" . . . for the battle is the Lord's, and he will give you into our hands" (I Samuel 17:47).

Jesus said, "Apart from me you can do nothing." And apart from His Words (the Bible) we will learn nothing about true living.

85

NOW TEST YOUR KNOWLEDGE

Answer true or false:

1. Our minds are computers with informational bits called thoughts.
2. Christians are expected to control their thoughts and emotions.
3. Anything can be accomplished by positive thinking.
4. We are to let our minds dwell on positive and useful thoughts.
5. David displayed an attitude of trust in God.
6. As a man thinks in his heart, so is he.
7. Material wealth is more important than wisdom and understanding.
8. The only source of wisdom is God.
9. Mindless Christianity is not Biblical Christianity.
10. All adults can mature in their thinking.

FOOD FOR THOUGHT

"So teach us to number our days, that we may apply our hearts unto wisdom."
—Psalm 90:12

11

LACK OF SELF-DISCIPLINE:
THE TOXIN OF MISMANAGEMENT
PROVERBS 6:6-10; 26:13-16; 31:10-31; JOHN 15:5;
I CORINTHIANS 9:24-27; PHILIPPIANS 3:10-24; 4:13;
I THESSALONIANS 5:21

Learn by Heart:
"The soul of the sluggard desireth, and hath nothing: but the soul of the diligent shall be made fat" (Proverbs 13:4).

EVERY DAY WITH THE WORD

Monday	The diligent	Proverbs 10:4; 12:24,27; 13:4; 21:5
Tuesday	The slothful	Proverbs 6:6-10; 15:19; 20:4; 24:30-34
Wednesday	A good example	Proverbs 31:10-31
Thursday	The possibility	Philippians 3:10-14
Friday	Developing discipline	I Corinthians 9:24-27
Saturday	Using time	Ecclesiastes 3:1-8
Sunday	Practicing discipline	John 15:1-8

Lack of self-discipline is just as much a toxin as greed, lying, or pride. Because of a lack of self-control, Christians fall victim to many of the enemy's temptations.

The Christian should not behave like a pinball, being the victim of everything he bounces against as he passes through life. Rather, like a diligent farmer, a trained athlete, and a good soldier, he should progress toward a goal. In order to become all that God wants us to be, and to do all that He would have us accomplish, we must mature in self-discipline.

DESIRING DISCIPLINE
(Proverbs 6:6-10; 26:13-16; 31:10-31)

The book of Proverbs paints a contrast between the lazy individual and the diligent. The lazy person does not get out and work, but rather lies around at home (Proverbs 26:13-15). He is also pictured as one who sleeps when he ought to work: "Yet a little sleep, a little slumber, a little folding of the hands to sleep." He is admonished to learn from the diligent ant (6:10).

A good illustration of someone who would exemplify self-discipline is the virtuous woman described in Proverbs 31. The woman is prized for her value (verse 10), and her husband is confident that he can rely on her (verses 11,12). She takes care of her routine activities, but she also is enterprising in business affairs. Notice the discipline in her daily schedule from the following verses: "She seeketh wool, and flax, and worketh willingly with her hands. She is like the merchants' ships; she bringeth her food from afar. She riseth also while it is yet night, and giveth meat to her household, and a portion to her maidens. She considereth a field, and buyeth it; with the fruit of her hands she planteth a vineyard. She girdeth her loins with strength, and strengtheneth her arms. She perceiveth that her merchandise is good: her candle goeth not out by night. She layeth her hands to the spindle, and her hands hold the distaff. She stretcheth out her hand to the poor; yea, she reacheth forth her hands to the needy. She is not afraid of the snow for her household: for all her household are clothed with scarlet. She maketh herself coverings of tapestry; her clothing is silk and purple. Her husband is known in the gates, when he sitteth among the elders of the land. She maketh fine linen, and selleth it; and delivereth girdles unto the merchant. Strength and honour are her clothing; and she shall rejoice in time to come. She openeth her mouth with wisdom; and in her tongue is the law of kindness. She looketh well to

"The hand of the diligent shall bear rule: but the slothful shall be under tribute" (Proverbs 12:24). Spiritual wealth, as well as physical well-being, are directly related to self-control.

Is it any wonder that her husband and children praise her? See verse 28.

the ways of her household, and eateth not the bread of idleness" (Proverbs 31:13-27).

While not everyone could master the work load of this remarkable woman, each of us can become self-controlled enough to handle the responsibilities God has given to us.

Self-discipline should be a natural characteristic of a believer's life. There are several reasons why Christians should grow in personal control. The first reason could be called the *freedom factor.* In Galatians 5:1 we read: "Stand fast therefore in the liberty wherewith Christ hath made us free, and be not entangled again with the yoke of bondage." Christ has delivered us from sin for a specific reason, and that is to honor Him with godly living. We have not been given freedom to vegetate but to actively follow the Lord. Self-discipline is essential to walk in obedience.

A second reason can be called the *balance factor.* Each of us has many responsibilities. It seems everybody has more things to do on their daily list than they can realistically accomplish. We have responsibilities to family, employers, neighbors, the church, and other individuals and organizations. Therefore it is essential that we become self-disciplined in order to maintain the necessary balance to fulfill our tasks.

Rather than responding to the loudest voice, our time should be divided in a balanced way to care for each area of our responsibility.

A third reason for developing self-control can be called the *time factor.* We are reminded that "it is required in stewards, that a man be found faithful (I Corinthians 4:2). God has a task for each one of us. Each of us has received an equal slice of time. It is equal in that we have 24 hours a day, but we do not know how many days have been allotted to us. Just as "today is the day of salvation," so also today is the day to be a disciplined, faithful steward.

A fourth reason to be self-disciplined can be called the *effectiveness factor*. Some people may enter a marathon just to receive a T-shirt, but most of the runners are interested in where they place in the race. "Know ye not that they which run in a race run all, but one receiveth the prize? So run, that ye may obtain" (I Corinthians 9:24). For the sake of freedom, balance, time and effectiveness, Christians must mature in self-discipline.

Self-discipline protects against laziness, but it also guards against impulsiveness. One may make a New Year's resolution without much thought about how to accomplish it. For others it may be the purchase of a new automobile they can't afford. For others it may be dining out too frequently because meals have not been planned in advance.

Godly self-discipline will protect you from slothfulness; it will also guard you against impulsiveness. Therefore, maturity and self-control are essential for each of us who belong to God.

Our desire is not just to accomplish a bunch of tasks, but it is to do a good job that will please the Lord.

The same lack of discipline that keeps people from selecting and accomplishing God's priorities for their lives makes them vulnerable to spurts of indiscriminate behavior.

DEVELOPING DISCIPLINE
(I Corinthians 9:24-27; Philippians 3:10-14; 4:13; John 15:5; I Thessalonians 5:21)

Good self-discipline is within reach for every child of God. Each believer can affirm the attitude of the Apostle Paul: "Brethren, I count not myself to have apprehended: but this one thing I do, forgetting those things which are behind, and reaching forth unto those things which are before, I press toward the mark for the

A desire to diligently press on in maturity begins with a passion to know Christ: "That I may know him, and the power of his resurrection, and the fellowship of his sufferings, being made conformable unto his death" (Philippians 3:10).

prize of the high calling of God in Christ Jesus" (Philippians 3:13,14). By making this statement Paul was admitting that he was not spiritually perfect. But he was not going to worry about past failures or rest on previous accomplishments. His goal was to grow in relationship to Christ, and in service to others. This should be our attitude as well.

Paul was so highly motivated and so well-disciplined that we have difficulty identifying with him. But, remember, in his same letter to the church at Philippi, Paul shared the reason behind his commendable attitudes and behavior. He said: "I can do all things through Christ which strengtheneth me" (Philippians 4:13). The emphasis in that sentence is not on the "I," but on the "through Christ which strengtheneth me." God has recorded His instructions in the Scriptures, and He provides opportunities each day to apply them. In addition, the Lord also strengthens us to be able to accomplish what He desires.

If we still need to be convinced that self-discipline is a real possibility for every believer, the words of Jesus recorded in John 15 should assure us: "I am the true vine, and my Father is the husbandman. Every branch in me that beareth not fruit he taketh away: and every branch that beareth fruit, he purgeth it, that it may bring forth more fruit. Now ye are clean through the word which I have spoken unto you. Abide in me, and I in you. As the branch cannot bear fruit of itself, except it abide in the vine; no more can ye, except ye abide in me. I am the vine, ye are the branches: He that abideth in me, and I in him, the same bringeth forth much fruit: for without me ye can do nothing. . . . Herein is my Father glorified,

To abide in Christ means to walk obediently after Him, studying His Word and confessing our sin when we have failed.

that ye bear much fruit: so shall ye be my disciples" (verses 1-5,8).

As the Christian remains in close relationship with Christ by following His Word, the Lord will produce fruit within him. Bible commentators agree that the fruit Christ referred to in John 15 is the fruit of the Spirit. This fruit is described in Galatians 5:22,23: "But the fruit of the Spirit is love, joy, peace, longsuffering, gentleness, goodness, faith, meekness, temperance: against such there is no law." The Christian will grow in love as he abides in Christ: he will deepen in peace and gentleness as he remains in close fellowship with the Saviour. In the same way his life will more and more be characterized by "temperance" (self-control) as he abides in Christ. Regardless of our background and predispositions, each of us can become more self-controlled as a result of abiding in Christ.

Our responsibility is to stay grafted into Jesus, and the fruit that He desires will be a byproduct of our relationship.

If we are to become faithful stewards, we must begin by examining our priorities. Since we do not have time to do everything, we must be selective in what we allow to become important in our lives. Too often we give attention to things that seem urgent yet are less important, while the significant things slip away. The Scripture exhorts us to live by priorities. Paul admonished: "Prove all things; hold fast that which is good" (I Thessalonians 5:21).

A simple way to examine our priorities is to make a list of all our responsibilities and activities. On the list we could place a "+" if the item needs more emphasis, a "−" if it should get less emphasis, an "X" if it should be eliminated, or a "*" if we are on target with the attention it is receiving. By eliminating a few items and re-

For example, a check of our daily schedules might reveal that washing the dishes and watching television are performed routinely each day, whereas the worship of God is frequently crowded out.

adjusting one or two others we will quickly be on our way to a deeper level of self-discipline.

A second practical help for growth in self-discipline is the use of a daily schedule to manage our time. We are conscious of the adversary's attack when we are tempted to lust or lie, but when we waste time throughout the day, we really don't think of that in relation to Satan. Paul's admonition to the Ephesians is also a warning to us: "See then that ye walk circumspectly, not as fools, but as wise, Redeeming the time, because the days are evil" (Ephesians 5:15,16). Poor planning is one of the most common time wasters. Therefore, if we follow a daily schedule we will accomplish more work and do a better job in our activities.

Contrary to thinking that our day begins in the morning, the Old Testament indicates that each new day begins in the evening. In the beginning of creation we read: "And the evening and the morning were the first day" (Genesis 1:5). Each evening before retiring we can take a few moments to schedule the new day's activities, and to evaluate the day just concluded. As we list phone calls that need to be made, letters to be written, people to be seen, items to be obtained, or things to be done, we can prayerfully ask the Lord to go before us and guide us so we will be effective ambassadors in those areas.

A non-believer can regulate his life according to this same procedure, but because he does not have the mind of Christ, for him it is just a behavioral technique. For the believer, the evaluation of daily activity and the setting up of the following day's schedule become spiritual acts. These activities may include a time of confession, thanksgiving, and dedication.

Daily planning books are available at stationery stores, or you could design your own schedule.

The Bible reminds us that we will be judged for our ministry as ambassadors. See II Corinthians 5:10-20.

Good self-discipline is essential for victory in Christian warfare. Some Christians are weak because they continually give in to Satan's temptation to complain. Others try to fight without strength because of prayerlessness. On the other hand, the adversary's assaults will be less effective against the Christian who is maturing in self-control. Paul said, "But I keep under my body, and bring it into subjection: lest that by any means, when I have preached to others, I myself should be a castaway" (I Corinthians 9:27). Paul did not want to be sidelined; he did not want to watch the game from the bench. His desire was to be where the action was, serving Christ with his whole heart.

Godly self-discipline helps the Christian against any temptation.

Who really wants to reap the results of impulsive behavior? What benefit is it to us or others if we slothfully lie around with low ambition? Rather, one day we can stand before our Lord as victors because of His grace, and because of our disciplined, Christ-honoring life.

Serving with our whole heart is the natural result of loving with our whole heart (Luke 10:27).

FOOD FOR THOUGHT

"O Lord, help us to be masters of ourselves, that we may be servants of others."
—Alexander Paterson

NOW TEST YOUR KNOWLEDGE

Answer true or false:

1. Some people just cannot be self-disciplined.
2. The diligent will be rewarded for their work.
3. Faithful stewards must be self-disciplined.
4. The Scripture warns against slothfulness and lack of discipline.
5. I can choose how I spend my own time.
6. The virtuous woman in Proverbs was impulsive.

Complete the following:

7. "See that ye walk circumspectly, not as fools, but as wise, _____ _____ _____ , because the days are evil."
8. "The soul of the _____ desireth and hath nothing: but the soul of the _____ shall be made fat."
9. "Prove all things; hold fast that which is _____ ."
10. "Brethren, I count not myself to have apprehended: but this one thing I do, _____ those things which are behind, and reaching forth unto those things which are _____ , I press toward the mark for the prize of the high calling of God in Christ Jesus."

12

I DID IT MY WAY:
THE TOXIN OF SELF-INDULGENCE
PSALM 37:1-11; ECCLESIASTES 1; 2; 4:1-3; MATTHEW
5:3-11; PHILIPPIANS 4:10-13

EVERY DAY WITH THE WORD

Monday	Futility of human wisdom	Ecclesiastes 1:2-8
Tuesday	Futility of materialism	Ecclesiastes 2:1-11
Wednesday	Despair	Ecclesiastes 2:11-20
Thursday	Delight and hope	Ecclesiastes 5:18-20
Friday	Delight	Psalm 37:1-11
Saturday	Hope	Titus 2:11-15
Sunday	Blessedness	Matthew 5:3-11

Learn by Heart: "And he said to them all, If any man will come after me, let him deny himself, and take up his cross daily, and follow me" (Luke 9:23).

The two wisest men who ever walked upon the face of the earth were King Solomon and Jesus of Nazareth. While they both had widely acclaimed reputations as wise teachers, their lifestyles were vastly different. Materially, Solomon had everything a person could desire, yet at the end of his life he felt empty. Jesus had nothing of worldly substance, yet His life was overflowing. The futility of a self-centered life results in despair, whereas a God-honoring life results in delight and hope. We can see the truth of this Scriptural principle as we take—

Solomon sought to please himself to do things his own way; Jesus sought to minister to others, to do things God's way.

A LOOK AT DESPAIR
(Ecclesiastes 1; 2; 4:1-3)

The writer of Ecclesiastes was probably King ‖

96

While divine inspiration preserved the king's thoughts, the process does not necessitate that all his conclusions were right.

The *Scofield Reference Bible* states that "vanity" does not refer to foolish pride, but "the emptiness and final result of all life apart from God."

Solomon. After a life of self-indulgence, he evaluated what was truly meaningful. His words in Ecclesiastes are often pessimistic, although occasionally he wrote with godly wisdom, as he did earlier in Proverbs. As Solomon wrote from his own vantage point, from a self-indulgent view, his conclusions were discouraging. But when Solomon mentioned God, and man's relationship to Him, a breath of hope characterized his words.

We can picture Solomon sitting with slumped shoulders; and having just exhaled deeply, he pens these words: "Vanity of vanities . . . vanity of vanities; all is vanity. What profit hath a man of all his labour which he taketh under the sun?" (Ecclesiastes 1:2,3). When a book begins by declaring everything is emptiness or futility, you know that the rest of the work will likely be pessimistic. Solomon continued in his lament by stating that people pass away, rivers never fill the sea, the eye is never satisfied with seeing, and there is nothing new taking place. The impression painted by the Preacher—Solomon—can be summarized: "Woe is me, for I want to taste more, but there are no new menus in life."

Solomon sought fulfillment through knowledge and wisdom. He wrote: "And I gave my heart to seek and search out by wisdom concerning all things that are done under heaven: this sore travail hath God given to the sons of man to be exercised therewith. I have seen all the works that are done under the sun; and, behold, all is vanity and vexation of spirit" (Ecclesiastes 1:13,14). After a life of pursuing wisdom and knowledge, King Solomon felt that the process was meaningless. While he learned much and was considered the wisest of men, his pursuit did not lead to satisfaction. Seeking wisdom was something that agitated and troubled him within. It failed to produce delight and peace.

Solomon also tried to find meaning in the pursuit of pleasure, so he indulged himself to the limit. But all his endeavors had a satiation point; and his thrill-seeking did not produce meaning. He admits: "I said in mine heart, Go to now, I will prove thee with mirth, therefore enjoy pleasure: and, behold, this also is vanity. I said of laughter, It is mad: and of mirth, What doeth it?" (Ecclesiastes 2:1,2).

Solomon next recorded how his pursuit of possessions and great accomplishments left him with an inner emptiness. "I made me great works; I builded me houses; I planted me vineyards: I made me gardens and orchards, and I planted trees in them of all kind of fruits: I made me pools of water, to water wherewith the wood that bringeth forth trees: I get me servants and maidens, and had servants born in my house; also I had great possessions of great and small cattle above all that were in Jerusalem before me: I gathered me also silver and gold, and the peculiar treasure of kings and of the provinces: I gat me men singers and women singers, and the delights of the sons of men, as musical instruments, and that of all sorts" (Ecclesiastes 2:4-8).

Solomon's self-centered living is summarized by his words, "And whatsoever mine eyes desired I kept not from them, I withheld not my heart from any joy; for my heart rejoiced in all my labour: and this was my portion of all my labour. Then I looked on all the works that my hands had wrought, and on the labour that I had laboured to

People often focus on what they do not have rather than on the many do: and, behold, all was vanity and vexation of spirit, and there was no profit under the sun" (Ecclesiastes 2:10,11). Everything that had once given Solomon pleasure seemed foolish to him at the end of his life. Everything that promised significance proved to be of little profit. At the end of his life he concluded that knowledge, pleasure, possessions, and accomplishments did not offer all they had promised.

The despair of self-centered living can also be seen in other places in the book of Ecclesiastes. Speaking out of self-pity, Solomon reflected on his finiteness (3:11), his ultimate fate (3:18-21), and widespread human oppression (4:1). Man's perceived smallness, in light of what takes place in the universe, led Solomon to this conclusion: "Wherefore I praised the dead which are already dead more than the living which are yet alive. Yea, better is he than both they, which hath not yet been, who hath not seen the evil work that is done under the sun" (4:2,3).

The depth of Solomon's despair is revealed by his words: "If a man beget an hundred children, and live many years, so that the days of his years be many, and his soul be not filled with good, and also that he have no burial; I say, that an untimely birth is better than he." The king felt a person was better off as a miscarriage than to lack sufficient resources. The king had it all, yet he felt empty!

What a contrast to the life of our Lord Jesus! Christ did not have any children, He did not live long, nor was He wealthy. He owned only the clothes on His back, traveled in a borrowed boat, and was buried in a borrowed tomb. However, no one ever accomplished more in life than Jesus did. Whereas Solomon said that everything was futility, Jesus demonstrated that even the smallest things in life can bring fulfillment.

What was the difference between Solomon and Jesus that resulted in such contrasting attitudes? Solomon, and more importantly our Lord, can give us insight as we take—

A LOOK AT DELIGHT AND HOPE (Psalm 37:1-11; Philippians 4:10-13; Matthew 5:3-11)

When Solomon looked at things from the how-everything-relates-to-me viewpoint, he concluded that life is futile. But when he snapped out of his self-centeredness and looked at his life in relation to a sovereign God, he recorded some accurate conclusions. For example, he wrote: "Every man also to whom *God hath given* riches and wealth, and hath given him power to eat thereof, and to take his portion, and to rejoice in his labour; this is *the gift of God.* For he shall not much remember the days of his life; because *God* answereth him in the joy of his heart" (Ecclesiastes 5:19,20). Work is meaningless just for work's sake. But when work is considered part of God's design for man, man can "rejoice in his labour." Whereas everything under the sun is vanity and vexation of spirit for the person who thinks only of himself, the person who recognizes God's presence knows "the joy of his heart."

If there was ever a message that contrasted sharply with the message of Ecclesiastes 2:1-11, it would be Matthew 5:1-12. The greatest sermon ever delivered by any preacher was not delivered in a sanctuary with stained glass windows. It was delivered by Jesus of Nazareth to a crowd

Self-pity is perhaps the leading source of depression.

In chapter 2 of Ecclesiastes, which expresses despair, the personal pronouns "I" and "me" appear repeatedly, but elsewhere, when Solomon relates life to God, hope is prevalent.

gathered on a hillside. The Sermon on the Mount gives a comprehensive description of meaningful living. The exhortations of the 61 verses of Matthew 5—7 can be summarized as: Be sensitive (5:1-12); Be an influence for good (5:13-16); Be a righteous practitioner (5:17-20); Be pure in thoughts, motives and words (5:21-37); Be gracious (5:38-48); Be private in devotions (6:1-18); Be free from things that possess (6:19-34); Be nonjudgmental (7:1-6); Be persistent in prayer (7:7-14); Be on your guard (7:15-23); and, Be doers of the Word (7:24-29).

At the beginning of His message, Jesus spoke of a life that would be richly rewarded. Rather than experiencing futility, emptiness, vanity, and vexation of spirit, a person can know fulfillment on earth and assurance of reward in Heaven. Listen to the ring of contrast through Ecclesiastes as Christ said: "Blessed are the poor in spirit: for theirs is the kingdom of heaven. Blessed are they that mourn: for they shall be comforted. Blessed are the meek: for they shall inherit the earth. Blessed are they which do hunger and thirst after righteousness: for they shall be filled. Blessed are the merciful: for they shall obtain mercy. Blessed are the pure in heart: for they shall see God. Blessed are the peacemakers: for they shall be called the children of God. Blessed are they which are persecuted for righteousness' sake: for theirs is the kingdom of heaven. Blessed are ye, when men shall revile you, and persecute you, and shall say all manner of evil against you falsely, for my sake. Rejoice, and be exceeding glad: for great is your reward in heaven: for so persecuted they the prophets which were before you" (Matthew 5:3-12).

A life of comfort, fulfillment, mercy, and reward is offered to those who are humble in their attitudes and seek after God with their whole heart. Solomon sought selfishly after things which pleased himself. He looked out for Number One. But self-centeredness leads to despair, and self-indulgence proves meaningless. There is always one more dream or one more possession that a person desires to grab, but when his hand is opened at the end of life, it is still empty. However, Jesus taught that a person who opens his hand to God and to others will find that more keeps falling into his hand. The natural man cannot understand this principle, but its truth is known to Christians.

Jesus reemphasized this lesson toward the end of His ministry. "And he said to them all, if any man will come after me, let him deny himself, and take up his cross daily, and follow me. For whosoever will save his life shall lose it: but whosoever shall lose his life for my sake, the same shall save it. For what is a man advantaged, if he gain the whole world, and lose himself, or be cast away?" (Luke 9:23-25).

The attitude Jesus showed was reflected centuries earlier in the Psalms. "Trust in the LORD, and do good; so shalt thou dwell in the land, and verily thou shalt be fed. Delight thyself also in the LORD; and He shall give thee the desires of thine heart. Commit thy way unto the LORD; trust also in him; and he shall bring it to pass" (Psalm 37:3-5). Delight and hope result from a right relationship with the Lord. They do not come about by pursuing selfish interests. The Apostle Paul understood this principle. His joy was not based

To pursue wisdom, knowledge, possessions, and great accomplishments, at the expense of being merciful, being pure in heart, or empathetic with the poor, is a rejection of the Lordship of Christ.

on circumstances. He wrote: " . . . I have learned, in whatsoever state I am, therewith to be content" (Philippians 4:11).

The enemy wants to persuade us to look out for ourselves, because, after all, no one else will, he suggests. But the Christian does not need to be duped by this. Meaning in life is derived from God. As we center our lives around Jesus Christ, we will be victorious over the adversary's toxin of self-indulgence.

NOW TEST YOUR KNOWLEDGE

Answer true or false:

1. Ecclesiastes shows us man's viewpoint apart from a relationship with God.
2. The activities of life have no ultimate meaning if man is an animal and there is no God.
3. Solomon knew that there was a God, but he frequently lived for his own pleasure.
4. Vanity, as used in Ecclesiastes, means life devoid of meaning.
5. Solomon expressed that work can have meaning, when it is understood in relationship to God.
6. Jesus taught that people find their lives when they are willing to lose them for His sake.
7. People had better indulge themselves now, because soon life will be over.
8. Selfish ambition is okay in some circumstances.
9. Self-denial is not really part of the Christian life.
10. An infinite number of satisfying years of living are a result of a few years of obedient living.

FOOD FOR THOUGHT

"Master selfishness or it will master you."
—Anonymous

13
THE BELIEVER'S HELPER:
THE HOLY SPIRIT
LUKE 4:1; ROMANS 8:1-27; EPHESIANS 5:18-21;
COLOSSIANS 3:16,17; HEBREWS 5:8; 9:14

EVERY DAY WITH THE WORD

Monday	Our need for help	Romans 7:7-24
Tuesday	Our Helper's identity	Romans 8:1,15
Wednesday	Our Helper's availability	Romans 8:16-27
Thursday	Our Helper's ministry	John 16:8-13
Friday	Our Helper's permanence	Ephesians 1:11-14
Saturday	Our Example of strength	Luke 4:1-13
Sunday	Our exercise of strength	Ephesians 5:18-21

Learn by Heart:
"And be not drunk with wine wherein is excess; but be filled with the Spirit" (Ephesians 5:18).

Who is the most powerful person in the world? If that question were asked of you, would you think of the country's wealthiest man? Would you think of the super powers, and believe it would be the leader of one of those countries? Actually, the most powerful person in the world is the Holy Spirit.

You say, "Wait a minute; that's not fair, because He's not really a person." Well, the Bible says He is. The Bible says the Holy Spirit has intellect; He knows our minds; and He knows the mind of God. He has emotions; we're told not to grieve the Holy Spirit. He has will; He gives gifts as He desires, as He determines. A person has intellect, emotion and will. The Holy Spirit is a person. And He is the most influential person in the world.

Our response to the Holy Spirit is different when we understand Him as a person rather than as a force.

THE BELIEVER'S SOURCE OF STRENGTH
(Romans 8:1-27)

This promise is found in John 14:16. There are two Greek words translated "another." This word means "exact likeness."

On the night before His death, Jesus told His disciples that He would send "another Comforter." He knew that He would be returning to the Father, but He also realized that the Holy Spirit would shortly be resident within each believer to help him. At His ascension Jesus told His disciples: "But ye shall receive power, after that the Holy Ghost is come upon you: and ye shall be witnesses unto me both in Jerusalem, and in all Judaea, and in Samaria, and unto the uttermost part of the earth" (Acts 1:8). The book of Acts is the record of the works of the Spirit in building the church.

Christians need the Holy Spirit, because in our own flesh we are powerless to be victors over sin. Paul's familiar struggle, mentioned in Romans 7, is the frequent experience of us believers. We are not immune to the failures described in the chapter. When we try to resist the adversary in our own strength, we are bound to fail.

Read Romans 7 and 8, noting the great contrast.

After Paul wrote the discouraging words of chapter 7, he penned the exciting words of chapter 8. What is the difference between the defeat in chapter 7, and the victory in chapter 8? The difference is the Holy Spirit. The power of the Holy Spirit is absent in chapter 7, whereas His influence permeates chapter 8.

The Holy Spirit is identified several times in Romans 8 by the term "the Spirit" (verses 8:1,4,5). He is also identified in chapter 8 as "the Spirit of life in Christ Jesus" (verse 2), "the Spirit of God" and "the Spirit of Christ" (verse 9), "the Spirit of him that raised up Jesus from the dead" (verse 11), and "the Spirit of adoption" (verse 15). This is the same Holy Spirit who was involved in the creation of the world (Genesis 1:2), the birth of Christ (Luke 1:35), and the new birth of each believer (John 3:3-6).

In our affluent corner of the world, we eat meal after meal without giving much thought to the process of getting that food to our tables. As we devour a pot roast, we rarely think of the farmer who grew the feed, the rancher who cared for the cattle, and the involvement of people in transportation, sales, federal inspection, butchering, packing, and preparation.

In the same way, Christians who are possessors of the greatest power in the universe, rarely stop to think about this valuable resource. While some understand the filling of the Holy Spirit, people seldom realize all that He does in the salvation process—past, present, and future.

Some people go to the other extreme, always thinking about the Spirit, and waiting for Him to do what God expects them to do in His power.

The Holy Spirit is involved in bringing people from unbelief to faith in Christ (John 3:3-6; 16:8-13). When they make a profession of faith, He immediately baptizes them into the body of Christ (I Corinthians 12:13), and secures their salvation (Ephesians 1:13,14).

After Paul explained the difficulty of holy living in our own strength (Romans 7), he showed in Romans 8 how the Holy Spirit ministers in every believer. He indwells and leads us. Paul explained: "But ye are not in the flesh, but in the Spirit, if so be that the Spirit of God dwell in you. Now if any man have not the Spirit of Christ he is none of his .... For as many as are led by the Spirit of God, they are the sons of God" (Romans

8:9,14). Notice how Paul mentioned that, if a person does not have the Holy Spirit, he is not a believer. All Christians are indwelt by the Spirit of Christ.

In Romans 8 we also notice that it is the Holy Spirit who gives us assurance. "The Spirit itself beareth witness with our spirit, that we are the children of God" (verse 16). While many Christians try to generate their own joy, peace, and love, it is the Spirit who produces fruit within us. The Holy Spirit produces these blessings and changes in us as we abide in Christ. When a Christian remains in a vital union with the vine, he bears much fruit (John 15:5). The fruit which the Holy Spirit produces "is love, joy, peace, longsuffering, gentleness, goodness, faith, meekness, and temperance" (Galatians 5:22,23). The sins of the flesh need not poison the child of God. Believers can be victors over these deadly toxins because the Holy Spirit helps them resist these practices and replace them with productive, Christ-honoring practices.

God has equipped His children with battle armor to resist the adversary. Ephesians 6 mentions how important the Word and prayer are in our wrestling with the adversary. However, there are times when we are so baffled that we are not even sure how to pray. Understanding our nature, God has also given us His Spirit to help us in this weakness. Paul wrote in Romans 8:26,27: "Likewise the Spirit also helpeth our infirmities: for we know not what we should pray for as we ought: but the Spirit itself maketh intercession for us with groanings which cannot be uttered. And he that searcheth the hearts knoweth what is the mind of the Spirit, because he maketh inter-

Review Ephesians 6:10-18.

cession for the saints according to the will of God."

The adversary is a super-human foe. The seven sons of Sceva learned that lesson the hard way. But the Christian can overcome the adversary, because the promise has been given: "Greater is he that is in you, than he that is in the world" (I John 4:4). Apart from Christ ministering through the indwelling Holy Spirit we can do nothing. But, with the Spirit's help we can do everything God wants us to do, and we can be everything God wants us to be. This is why Paul could pray so confidently for the Ephesian Christians to "be strengthened with might by his Spirit in the inner man" (Ephesians 3:16).

See Acts 19:14-17.

THE BELIEVER'S USE OF STRENGTH (Ephesians 5:18-21; Luke 4:1; Hebrews 5:8; 9:14; Colossians 3:16)

After Paul explained to the Ephesians the importance of putting off the old man and putting on the new man, he gave another contrast which illustrates the Holy Spirit's role in the process. "And be not drunk with wine, wherein is excess; but be filled with the Spirit" (Ephesians 5:18). Christians are not to be under the influence of anything . . . they are to be under the influence of the Holy Spirit. Victory comes as we follow the leading of the Holy Spirit.

We can see the importance of the ministry of the Holy Spirit when we study the life of the Lord Jesus. From Luke's Gospel we recognize that Jesus was conceived by the Holy Spirit (1:35), filled by the Holy Spirit (4:1), and anointed by the Holy Spirit (4:18). When the Pharisees accused

Christ of performing His miracles by the power of Satan, He stated that even His casting out of devils was by the Spirit of God (Matthew 12:28). At the beginning of His ministry Jesus followed the Spirit even into battle with the adversary; and at His death He offered Himself to God by the Spirit (Hebrews 9:14). If the Son of God in His earthly life relied on the leading and strength of the Holy Spirit, surely we must trust His leading and depend on His strength for obedient living.

The contrast in Ephesians 5:18 is to not be under the influence of wine but under the influence of the Holy Spirit. Rather than letting alcohol influence, guide or control our behavior, we must let the Holy Spirit direct, guide and influence our behavior. Whereas all Christians are baptized once by the Holy Spirit at the time of their salvation, the filling of the Holy Spirit is a continual experience. Literally, the command means to be continually being filled with the Holy Spirit.

The Greek word for fill is *pleroo*. A full understanding of that word can help us realize what it means to follow the Holy Spirit's leading. *Pleroo* means "to accomplish" or "to be complete." At Pentecost the Christians were filled with the Holy Spirit; they saw accomplished within themselves the fulfillment of Christ's promise. The Spirit draws people to Christ, regenerates them, baptizes them into the body, perseveres in their behalf, and seals them unto the day of redemption. A full salvation has been accomplished and is the completed position of every believer.

The word can also be translated "to satisfy or to be fulfilled." Christians understand the joy of their salvation, and as they fellowship with Christ

> There is a difference between the Holy Spirit's taking residence in a believer, and His having full leadership in that life every moment.

> "And ye are complete in him, which is the head of all principality and power" (Colossians 2:10).

they sense a deep satisfaction. Whereas people in the world may seek fulfillment through pleasure, materialism, or entertainment, the Christian knows a contentment apart from externals. God is accomplishing His best will in the life of His children, and as the Christian is filled with the Holy Spirit he experiences this satisfaction and fulfillment.

Pleroo can also be translated "to cram, or to furnish." These two words are very picturesque. The first pictures a container that is packed to capacity. When we are filled with the Holy Spirit we are crammed with His holiness, goodness, truth, love, righteousness and faithfulness. The Holy Spirit is to have a complete occupancy of our lives. He needs to be able to settle down and feel at home in our hearts, and completely furnish our lives.

The home of a newly married couple is not likely to be pleroo (filled). But the home of an elderly couple, especially if they have retired to a smaller home, is likely to be "thoroughly furnished."

Pleroo can also mean "to be thoroughly influenced." There are many individuals and organizations that would like to influence us. There are many things that seek our attention and affection. The issue is not whether we will be influenced or not influenced, whether we'll be controlled or not controlled; the issue is to what influence we will submit ourselves. The Christian is responsible for how he lives his life. The last item mentioned in the fruit of the Spirit (Galatians 5:22,23) is self-control. Sometimes we hear that the Holy Spirit controls us. It is more accurate to say that the Holy Spirit will lead and empower the believer as he exercises godly self-control. Day by day we exercise our control to follow His full influence.

We use our will to follow His will.

How the Holy Spirit influences our lives can be understood from Paul's parallel statements in

Ephesians and Colossians. In Ephesians 5:18 we are commanded to be filled with the Holy Spirit, and then verses 19 through 21 show the result of being filled. By way of reminder, the text tells us "Speaking to yourselves in psalms and hymns and spiritual songs, singing and making melody in your heart to the Lord; Giving thanks always for all things unto God and the Father in the name of our Lord Jesus Christ; Submitting yourselves one to another in the fear of God" (Ephesians 5:19-21). In Colossians 3:16 Paul tells us to "let the word of Christ dwell in you richly in all wisdom; teaching and admonishing one another in psalms and hymns and spiritual songs, singing with grace in your hearts to the Lord." The filling of the Holy Spirit occurs, then, as the word of Christ dwells in us richly.

> Just as the Holy Spirit fills in response to the believer's petition, so He fills in response to the Christian's committed study of the Scriptures.

In both contexts we see how the Spirit and the Word influence our relationship with God (praise and thanksgiving), our relationship with ourselves (inner joy), and our relationship to one another (submission). Paul is not speaking about two things that produce this result, but one and the same thing. How do we experience the filling of the Holy Spirit? By allowing the Word of Christ to dwell in us. By letting the Word of God satisfy us, be our fulfillment, cram and furnish our minds and thoroughly influence us.

The adversary desires to keep unbelievers from the truth of the gospel. He also works hard at hindering Christians from glorifying God and experiencing fulfillment in Christ. He uses the toxins of guilt, envy, or complaining against some Christians. Some he attacks with pride, lying or greed. With others he's more silent, attempting to defeat them through prayerlessness. But we can be wise to his warfare; his toxins need not harm us. The Scriptures promise ultimate victory, and they offer daily victory as we abide in Christ. Those who recognize the adversary's toxins, and who rely in the strength of the Holy Spirit to overcome those toxins, will be the victors.

Remember... "Greater is he that is in you, than he that is in the world" (I John 4:4).

NOW TEST YOUR KNOWLEDGE

Match the following:

1. The believer's need for strength
2. The regeneration of the Holy Spirit
3. The filling of the Holy Spirit
4. The sealing of the Holy Spirit
5. The intercession of the Holy Spirit

A. Ephesians 1:13,14
B. Romans 8:26,27
C. John 3:3-6; 16:8-13
D. Ephesians 5:18-21
E. John 15:5; Romans 7

Answer true or false:

6. Some Christians have not been baptized by the Holy Spirit.
7. The Holy Spirit produces fruit in believers.
8. Jesus led His life in submission to the Holy Spirit.
9. Even when we don't know how to pray the Holy Spirit helps us.
10. Being filled with the Holy Spirit is the same as letting the words of Christ thoroughly permeate our minds and actions.

FOOD FOR THOUGHT

"I should as soon attempt to raise flowers if there were no atmosphere, or produce fruits if there were neither light or heat, as to regenerate men if I did not believe there was a Holy Ghost."

—Henry Ward Beecher